Flowers &
Elephants

Flowers & Elephants

CONSTANCE SITWELL

A Voyage through India

Foreword by **E.M. Forster**

An imprint of
Natraj Publishers
Dehradun • New Delhi

Text copyright © Natraj Publishers

About Constance Sitwell © John and Ann Ferguson

First Published in 1927
Reprinted 2012

ISBN 978-81-8158-108-2

Published by Mrs. Veena Arora for Etch, an imprint of
Natraj Publishers, Publications Division, Dehra Dun
and printed at Saurabh Printers Pvt. Ltd., New Delhi

NOTHING CAN BE LIKE
THE EAST BUT ITSELF.

– *The author's Journal*
1912

FOREWORD

A FLOWER from the tree of life was given to Adam and Eve when they were expelled from Paradise. It had no magic force, it was only a flower which had not ripened into fruit and the bestowal of immortality, they could not eat of it. Still, it was all they had to remind them of their garden, and as they wandered over the earth, engendering the future emotions of mankind, they gazed at it through tear-blurred eyes. Sometimes it seemed to them merely a flower; beautiful, valuable, unique, but no more: and from that vision was born what we in our modern jargon call the 'Western point of view.' To the Westerner, be he artist or merchant, a flower is usually a flower, an elephant is an elephant, and a diamond a diamond; objects to the Westerner remain real and separable: they can be understood and described, they can be possessed or sold. But at other times Adam and Eve saw their flower differently. Its petals swelled, it became heavy and grey, and behold! it had expanded into an elephant. Or it shrank and shone, and lo! it was a diamond. These changes in its nature increased their sadness, for

[7]

they did not know which of the changes would be permanent. And from their doubt was born what we now call the 'Indian point of view'; to the Indian nothing is real and nothing is separable: elephants and flowers and diamonds all blend and are part of the veil of illusion which severs unhappy mortals from the truth.

These two views, the Western versus the Indian, practical versus mystic, by no means complete our spiritual inheritance. Our forefathers had a third vision. At certain moments their flower seemed a flower as far as it went, and the elephant as far as he went was an elephant, but nothing went far enough. Things were separate, they were real, but oh so imperfect; they had not their full essence, they only contained hints. At what did they hint? At God? Not directly. Each suggested its own absent perfection – that is all that one could say. The flower said, 'There is the topmost blossom on the tree of life, unspoiled by human fingers.' The elephant said, 'There is a huge and happy beast in the jungles of Eden whom men shall never humiliate or trap.' The diamond said, 'There is a jewel beyond price and greed, safe in the treasure-house of the Father.' Plato was one of the inheritors of this third vision and the writer of this book has inherited it also.

She possesses it, not as a system or a philosophy, but as a gift. To her, as to Plato, the world is real – as far as it goes; it is as she sets it forth in her simple and profound prologue: a marriage feast to which the bridegroom has not yet come. 'I will be the bridegroom!' cry the gallant Englishmen. Poor young fellows, how can they be? They can no more involve her in their certainties than she can involve them in her dream.

It is necessary to emphasize this aspect of Mrs. Sitwell's book, for the reason that it is not at all the book it seems to be. Misled by its unpretentiousness, the careless reader will mistake it for the travel impressions of a young lady who went to stop with her brother in India, where she had one or two proposals of marriage which she declined. Our heroine visits Bombay and the Taj, she includes Ceylon, she attends Brigade Sports and an elephant drive, she peeps at maharajahs and bazaars and idles in clubs, she sympathetically repels the attentions of elderly men. She is charming. How well one knows it all! But the book is not like that. An indwelling spirit informs it, and the colour of a sea voyage, the vivid touches of oriental life, the clever snatches of talk, are bound together and heightened by that contest between perfection and imperfection which runs through all the Platonic vision. Life is at one moment so exquisite and near, at the next worthless and remote. Despondency and happiness succeed each other as swiftly as the motions of a parrot's wing, and happiness is more probable in solitude. So the girl strives to be alone, not – as some women – in order that she may enhance her attractiveness, but in order that she may achieve her vision. At the end, when she is home again, and the marvels and disquiets of her Indian tour are composing themselves, she finds hope and peace: 'I knew there was permanence: I felt reality. I shall find them, I said to myself, the flowers and jungles and innocent huge beasts. I shall find them where the pattern of these things eternally dwells.'

Mrs. Sitwell has known India well, and has filled her pages with many vivid little pictures, and with sounds and scents. But it is the thread on which her impressions are strung that has fascinated me, a thread so delicate and rare that the least clumsiness in definition will snap it. While trying to write this Foreword I have indeed felt like that 'thick middle-aged man who was generally very active and lively,' and who leant over the steamer rail by her side and expected to acquire her soul in the course of five minutes. My excuse is that I may have hinted to the discriminating reader what not to look for in *Flowers and Elephants*. It is not a young lady's portfolio of travel sketches. Still less is it a love story.

E. M. FORSTER

AFGHANISTAN

KASHMIR

PUNJAB

BALUCHISTAN

Bahawalpur

RAJPUTANA

UNITED
PROVIN

SIND

Cutch

CENTRAL

CENTRAL PROV

Kathiawar

Tropic of Cancer

BOMBAY

A R A B I A N

HYDERABAD
NIZAM'S DOMINIONS

S E A

MADRAS

MYSORE

Laccadive
Islands

THE INDIAN EMPIRE
PREPARED FOR
THE IMPERIAL GAZETTEER OF INDIA

Scale 1 : 10,000,000 or 157 Miles to an inch

Nine Degree Channel

Eight Degree Channel

Maldive
Islands

Cape Comorin

FLOWERS
AND ELEPHANTS

I

EVERYTHING was heightened for me that day –
the earth soaked with colour, and my
thoughts steeped in emotion. Perhaps it was the
idea of going away for some time and leaving it all
that made me think I had never seen the slopes and
glades of the park look more beautiful. It was
afternoon, a sunny autumn veil hung over everything. The massed woods in the distance were
rich russet and blue; the beeches rose in the chill
and shining air, their fiery leaves burning fierce-
coloured in the last rays of the sun. They held
their sweeping boughs of orange and yellow high
poised across the way, and below lay spread the
bright copper carpet of their leaves. Between the
smoothness of their trunks the road wound along,
and on the short grass all round the fallow-deer
vaguely, lightly wandered.

The hollows and little valleys in the park were
brimming up with bluish mist; above them the
house, long and grey, stood at the top of the hill.

I drove slowly up to it, loath to leave this still outside world that smelt of autumn leaves and damp freshness; but it was growing dark, the deer in front of the house were half lost in the dusk.

A footman stood by the great door of the hall, looking out. We were all collecting there for a dress-rehearsal of the little play that was to be acted for the village people at Christmas. But we scarcely thought of that now, we were so interested in each other and in the fun of meeting. I was to be the village bride in the play. As I came in the footman told me that the others had arrived already, and were changing for the rehearsal that was to be after tea.

The hall lost its height in dim shadows at the top; I went alone up the white stone stairs leading to the shining passages and galleries. There was a big fire burning in my room, the curtains and the counterpane of the high canopied bed were silk of a lovely blue, and on it was spread a froth of white muslin and lace – my play-bridal dress. It was a Victorian dress of billowy flounces; a lace veil hung over a chair, and on the floor beside it were old satin shoes with big rosettes. The room was lit by candles only, its corners were all in shadow, but the polished furniture and bed-posts caught the leaping light of the fire, and the blue silk gleamed.

I changed, dressing very carefully, and then went across to the long glass to look. It was very quiet in the room. I saw myself all white against the dark background and suddenly I was filled with an odd foreboding. In our play the bridegroom never appeared. The bride was foolish, constantly changing her mind; the bridegroom, always on the point of coming, was never actually seen; and, as I stood there, I had a superstitious feeling that this play was a forecast of what would happen to me in my own life. I seemed to lose all sense of where I was, and felt all at once as though I stood inside a globe and saw the wheel of time turning. I saw myself starting off to travel about the world, going from place to place in a sort of dream, people passing vaguely, but no one staying clearly in my mind, and when I got round the circle I was again alone. 'Well, never mind,' I said to myself, 'the earth is full of lovely things, and I shall see them – rivers and temples and exotic flowers! Perhaps I shall wear those flowers,' I went on in a confused fashion, 'instead of any bridal wreath, and perhaps I shall like them just as well!'

I tried to shake myself clear of these thoughts,

but when I went downstairs again I felt clouded and hesitant, as though I were going to meet some dimly-felt crisis. The house might have been empty it was so noiseless. In my white clothes I went along the polished echoing passages as softly as a ghost until I reached the library door. Standing there, I could hear the voices inside, and the sound of the tea-cups and the people laughing.

I still felt as though I were half in the future, and paused for some time with my hand on the door-handle before turning it and going in. The long room, lit by lamps, was filled by the big party who were having tea. Lamplight and fire-light fell warm on the orange curtains hanging in thick folds over the tall windows, and shone on the gilt lettering of the books that lined all the walls of the room. Under one of the lamps was a large bunch of dahlias; smoky crimson, deep red, and marvellous tawny yellow. There were three or four tables of tea-things, with the party clustering round them; they were all dressed up in rich old clothes, dark blue and claret and brown; the scene reminded me of some dusky picture by a Venetian painter.

The heavy door shut softly behind me, and I stood there unnoticed, looking at them all laughing and talking. Jack was standing at the far end of the room getting some tea. I saw him directly I came in; and he saw me. His eyes dwelt on mine with a sort of surprise, as though some new thing were dawning on him against his will. We stared at each other across the others, each of us gazing as if at a stranger. It was no more than a moment really, I suppose, but it seemed a long time.

His head stood out distinctly against the book-lined wall – his hard young face, with its rather dissipated and dare-devil look that went oddly with the quietness of his eyes, set widely apart. Again he made me feel as though I were a ghost, and I moved uneasily towards the others, who at last noticed me; and then Margaret called out: 'The Bride! Here she is! – Oh, isn't she a Kate Greenaway bride!' Then they all turned round and looked at me, and some one began clapping. As I walked across to a sofa, I felt a little dazed, and my hands trembled so I could hardly hold the cup of tea that Jack brought me. He gave me a wondering look, took the cup from me again, and put it on the table near by. After this he went across to the fireplace and lit a cigarette. I talked to Margaret a little while, then Jack came back.

'Are you excited at the thought of going out to India?'

'I never really like any change,' I answered. 'I

hate to think of life passing and changing. There is so much. . . . I can't even keep pace with the ordinary life of every day, and all the fun.'

'You sound like the child in that poem of Coleridge's, who "always finds and never seeks," ' he said, and then, as I remained silent, with a little laugh he went on: 'Things fall, you know, into quite another pattern in India.'

'But I like the pattern of things here,' I murmured.

He asked me of our plans, and I told him that the people I was to travel with were almost strangers; but that when I arrived I would stay with my brother, who had been away in the East for three years now. Jack's manner still made me feel a little shy, but I said at the end:

'And I suppose I shall see you, too, out there?'

'You will –' he assented, 'unless the regiment is moved; or unless there is a war; or unless I am dead. But – oh, you'll make plenty of new friends.'

'Anyhow,' I answered, smiling, 'you are part of the life I'm used to; and that is what I like. We have known each other for a good many years now, haven't we?'

'Yes,' he said, and turned away to stare into the fire.

After this there was a silence, and other people came and talked; but later on – after the play was over – Jack approached me again and said:

'I feel that you are a different person this evening, dressed up in those things! You have become different, almost grown-up, for once.'

'Don't you like it – the dress?' I asked – 'this dear old muslin spread round in frills? I feel like a story-book person in it.'

'Oh, yes, it's lovely,' he agreed. 'But you are like a story-book person – always.' I thought his voice had a certain bitterness.

'Well! what harm is there in that?'

He shrugged his shoulders. 'Fairy-stories are not very satisfying. However,' he went on, 'even princesses in fairy-stories fall in love – sooner or later.'

I laughed and said as lightly as I could, 'Well, for this princess it will be later – much later – if ever at all.'

His voice hardened as he replied: 'You can't have *everything* your own way in this world. But you haven't learnt that yet, have you? You manage to live in a world of your own making; it's too much of a dream altogether.'

'It's a happy world, anyhow,' I retorted, 'and that is something.'

'May it continue!' said he; 'but remember that other people have to come into it who may not be so happy – and who may want more,' he finished shortly.

He threw his cigarette into the fire and held out his hand to say good-bye. His face had a look of impatience on it, and although the little play had gone off very well and I was feeling quite exhilarated, my sense of foreboding returned. I could not help wondering whether I was right to live in my own world, and be so happy.

II

I CAN hear the swish of the sea now as I write,
and the quiet noise of the waves on each side of
the ship as we go so very smoothly along through
the Gulf of Suez. If one listens one can hear and
feel the pulse and vibration of the engines, though
very faintly. It is the luncheon hour; I am almost
alone on deck. There are some Lascars rolling up
the awnings in front of me; their bare feet clench
the railings on which they stand; the lithe figures
in fluttering indigo and their bare brown legs are
dark against the sparkling sea.

I do want, while I travel, to write of the unforgettable little spaces of time that come when
imagination is merged into living in a special way,
and the thing seen becomes like a work of art,
intense, significant, separate. They come suddenly, these perfect moments of perfect life, and
they remain with me for ever. If of all the places
that lie before me I can see even one in that way I
shall think of it as mine, mine – safe in my secret
world.

We reached Suez before the sun rose to-day. I
got up very early; the morning sparkled – the sea
shimmering the palest green and blue; and Suez
lay, just a low line of ochre and lilac buildings,

along the yellowish shore. In the cool air lovely bird-like boats, painted green, with pointed white sails came sailing near and about us. The huddled figures in them seemed to have been there all night, so immobile were they; while one steered the others sat, with blue cloths shrouding them, silently looking across the water. Some of the boats brought slippery fish, some dates crushed into blocks, some fruit piled high. It was very quiet. All the colour was cool, clear and light, there were no dark shadows; and I walked about the wet, washed decks by myself, so happily.

But when the sun rose everything altered suddenly, and lost the quality of dream: the men in the boats bestirred themselves and began talking; other passengers appeared, Lascars ran pattering about the ship with their hard, light tread, the houses on shore shone white with deep shadows, and more boats came rowing out towards us; boats full of boys, brown and black, clothed in a few wisps, who sang and grinned with white teeth, and rowed slowly round the ship, their faces upturned while they shouted their guttural Arabic to one another. The boats bobbed about jauntily on the sunny little waves that lapped the steep side of the ship. In one of them sat a blue-black Nubian youth with a bit of pink stuff knotted round his head; his gleaming body looked polished in its blackness against the pale water as he sprawled there idly with a parrot perched on his shoulder.

And now we are passing by the ridged coast of Arabia, where the cobalt and amethyst ledges curve against the vacant sky so sharply that the mountains might be cut sapphires flawed with deeper azure.

Most of the life on a ship is ordinary enough between the meals that heavily divide the day. I have plenty of time to think of all the new places I shall see. I think too of Jack; I think of him with a sort of fear, for again he will make me feel that I am too indefinite. He wants to break into my dreams, and I still love my own world in which I must be alone. For when I am not alone those miraculous moments never come to me, solitary moments lit with what must surely be a kind of insight and made permanent by their completeness. All other things belong to time and so quickly pass away.

And yet it is actually through Jack's mind that I see some places, little though I want to. Port Said, for instance, that rubbish heap! We got there at night when the lighthouse was waving its swords of light in large sweeps about the sky; and

later on we landed. There was no traffic in the
white road, deep in dust; the unreal-looking
houses stuck up abruptly out of the sand. There
is no noise of feet there, only the bead-sellers'
chatter and the plump pallid shopmen talking at
their open doors.

We went to a jaded-looking café in a colonnade,
and sat at one of the little marble tables to drink
coffee. A bright white light from strong lamps
fell on the big-leaved dry plants in tubs below, all
powdered with white dust, and on the parched
road, and on an acrobat in silver tights, who stood
on his head and walked on his hands up and down
the untidy street. The light glittered on his waving silver legs and stiff arms, and near by there
lounged a dingy Dago band playing frail tunes.
A sallow little girl in a dirty pink dress stood in
the harshest glare singing mechanically in a worn
voice; all the squalor, all the sordidness, of the
place seemed embodied in that poor little creature,
so sleepless and unwashed. Jack loathes Port
Said, I thought. And no wonder! How smirched
everything is there! But I am not sure that most
things don't look rather hard and arid seen
through his cold eyes.

Never mind! all that has been blown away by
the wind now. I stood in the bows of the ship in

the evening as we went down the Canal after coaling at Port Said. The sun had set over the desert, leaving a saffron and daffodil sky of curious flatness, with rosy clouds flung across it. I could just hear a gramophone playing on deck for the people to dance to, but the desert was tense with the unmistakable silence of the East.

After a while one of the passengers, a thick middle-aged man, who was generally very active and lively, came up and leant on the rail at my side. It was bright moonlight; the white paint of the ship had a silvery look, even the ropes sloping high above us seemed of twisted silver. There were stars, too, in spite of the moon, and cool serenity, but a hot wind blew strongly between the high peace of sky and limitless sand. Its force was tremendous; I had to cling to my pale silk skirts, and the bit of gauze around my head blew round and round high above me.

'Won't you come back to the main deck,' said he, 'where the wind is not so strong?'

I hesitated; not only do people dislike solitude for themselves, I thought, but they seem to dislike it for others as well. I answered that I liked standing here where it was quiet and thinking of the desert stretching away and away into Africa.

He smiled, as if he thought this rather a joke.

[27]

He would have thought it still more of a joke,
I suppose, if I had told him what I was imagining:
miles of colourless sand lying pale under the
moon, and sand-coloured lions moving; and fields
of blue vetch by the Nile; and the black tombs of
the bulls of Apis, dark and stifling under their
load of sand – thick heat in there, and thick darkness, and the empty sombre passages going between the great black granite tombs, sunk deep in
underground halls. And fields of beans, and fields
of lupins and loose-growing sugar-cane and dense
corn; and behind, the rosy wall of the Libyan
mountains in the jocund morning light, honey-
combed with tombs – full of mummies in hard
painted cases; and painted halls and creamy passages, and roofs coloured with the young blue of
Egypt – the most adorable colour in the world.

'Come and dance on deck,' he said cheerfully.
'That's what you should be doing at your time
of life.'

I think he felt it was a duty to rouse me from
melancholy thoughts; and I couldn't see how to
undeceive him. At last rather stupidly I said:
'Did you see the lilac jelly-fish this morning?
And the sea-snakes diving amongst them?'

'No,' he answered, laughing and staring. And
his stare seemed to say: 'You're a queer girl cer-

tainly. But you'll change all right as you grow older; you'll find ordinary things are the best in the end – and the good old ordinary way of living.'

We stood silent for a little; the bright light of the ship fell on the low banks of the Canal, and on a man, hooded like a monk, who sat in a little boat moored by the side: he had lighted a small fire in his boat and was sitting motionless watching a cooking-pot, not even glancing up at the high sides of the ship as it glided, all lit and towering, by.

'He seems as self-absorbed as I am,' I said, pointing to the lonely crouching figure.

I laughed, but my companion looked a little cross and walked off, whilst I also felt a little cross at being thought foolish and sentimental.

'How delicious it is to be alone!' I said to myself stubbornly, and quoted Emily Brontë:

'I'll walk where my own nature will be leading,
It vexes me to choose another guide.'

Some of the crew were sitting about in the fo'c'sle talking lazily and singing scraps of songs. I looked up at the mast with the dull orange light at its tip moving smoothly along amid the maze of twinkling stars. The warm wind blowing across

Africa made the ropes hum and blew my hair about. Moonlight flooded all the wide expanse. And dreamily I thought again of the morning's amazing sight, for as I was looking over the ship's side into the sun-filled purity of clear blue water, I saw it starred with thousands, with countless multitudes, of jelly-fish. Floating there in the fields of the sea, all misty lilac, half transparent and half opaque, swayed this way and that in the limpid waves, they moved gently, seeming tranced by the slow motion. Tremulous, with filaments of palest mauve spreading round them and wavering in the warm sea, they stretched as far as eye could see right down into the translucent blue.

And then as I looked I suddenly saw, plunging deeply amongst the soft nebulous forms, two glistening sea-snakes. Shining emerald they were; swift and twisting they seemed to reel downwards to the depths. I felt that I was looking into a world of life too remote, too strange, too fantastic, and I looked no longer, half afraid that some still greater marvel would appear.

III

AFTER the jangling noise of Bombay, with its vivid shifting crowds that pour down every street; after its confused mixed life and the confused pungent scents that trail about; after the wondrous evening light there that gathers itself together and seems to splash everything with ruddy gold, here, where everything has the unfamiliar note of Central Asia, we seem to be on the very bones of the world – rocky spines and ribs of flint and granite.

Through the winter the bones have been naked, stark and massive except for a few severe lines of snow down the sides of the mountains. So now that the spring has come, and this world is putting on some coverings, we feel them really to be embroidery and bright ornaments. First come the grape hyacinths, standing stiffly, little blue armies of them, amongst the trees. Then the apricots and almonds, tossing their blossoms in the wind, curiously fragile looking with the steely mountains for a background. And then we saw the desert ground being covered more and more thickly with twisted leaves, and from them rose slender yellow tulips. The mountains too brought forth living things: the long trains of camels pass-

ing through the brown defiles have a look as of
giving out amber light; the black and white sheep
seem more distinct, more vigorous yet. There is
more of a lilt in the walk of these Mongolian
beggars, dressed in dirty pink rags.

Yes, the passionate wind of the spring blows
here too – more poignantly even than in England.
It is so very short-lived, this Eastern spring! See
how quickly the flowers are shrivelling up! The
soft breathing and blowing makes one catch one's
breath at men's transitoriness. The sense of that
nearly withered me yesterday – more humble and
fleeting than ever I feel.

We had ridden out of the town into a wide
valley with dun and ochre hills all round. The
others had gone forward to see a gorge farther on,
so I sat by a rock and waited for them while the
dusk fell. All about were pitched the tents of
travelling tribes, who are shepherds. Their tents
are black, or striped black and brown. They
looked so sudden on the pale ground. In this
place is no abiding home for men – only the black
tents, and on all sides the moving masses of sheep
– cream-coloured blotches on the earth. The
shepherds were calling them together to fold
them in from the wolves and jackals. Children
herded the lambs, carrying green branches in their

hands; the little lambs were amazingly white, but there were some with black markings. The shepherds' voices calling filled that still brown valley, and the sheep answered bleating. The evening was full of the bleating of sheep, and the weaker bleating of lambs. I said to myself this coarse grass that I have picked is the same as grew in the time of David, also a shepherd boy; these same sounds that I am hearing fell on the ears of Esau in his rough clothing; and perhaps Abel, a keeper of sheep, heard just this calling on his last evening on earth. The rock I am leaning against is still hot from the sun that has beaten on it all day, just as it was at this hour a thousand years ago.

Is this the sort of rock that Jacob slept on, I wondered, when it had cooled in the night? I wish an angel would appear now—flaming pointed wings against that peaked mountain behind.

How lovely the solitude was – a sort of ecstasy to me, like Blake's 'eternity in an hour'. Amazing skies seen alone! And as the sense of loneliness deepens all things become symbolic – the bent head of the shepherd; the boy playing his pipe by the smooth stones of the stream – timeless and ageless they appear.

One of the first things I saw after we arrived here was a wedding procession. We were driving through a bit of country where the ground was white with asphodel. The pale flowers were lit up like thistle-down by the low rays of the sun; they glistened like desert foam. Leagues of them – so light and white; legions of ghosts of flowers it seemed; and through them came the wedding procession. It was led by a man in a brown coat with squares of vivid orange let in, like a dancer in a Russian ballet; and then came a camel bearing the bride in a palanquin. The whole erection was covered with a pale lilac curtain. I couldn't see the bride; it looked as if she were a caged bird being carried slowly away. Behind her there was noise and gaiety – a line of black oxen with weather-stained pink cloths thrown over them, and ridden by women in the heaviest, most gorgeous colours – unrelieved crimson and blue and red. Can you see how definite, how sensual they looked in that shimmering expanse of white, and how the short steps of the oxen went after the slow swinging of the high camel? At the end of the little party were donkeys with yellow bundles slung across their backs, and some young men beating tom-toms. The young men were beautiful, all in white, with dark long hair and beards; they smiled at us as they passed. I hoped the helpless bride was to be given to some one like them.

How unexpected are the things here! -- the men sit in their shops and drink, out of brightly-coloured Russian china, tea made in samovars. The animals are herded by men in sheep-skins. Thibetan holy men, in stained and faded rags, wander about, often smiling in an idiotic, happy way. Their broad, dirty faces are made for smiling, surely. The shops are piled up with rugs from Bokhara, and soft cat-skins and fox-skins. The air is very keen and crystal clear; the plane trees, white against those sapphire mountains streaked with shadows, make an avenue straight up the chief street of the Bazaar. The first time we went along it I stopped suddenly where the copper-smiths were hammering, for I saw, set along a low wooden form, a row of pots painted pale red, and in them cyclamen. My heart was caught up with delight. Dear cyclamen, I thought—dear mixture of lilac and red; you feel so much my own, I must throw a greeting to you in this strange place.

One day the lady doctor at the Mission Hospital asked me to go with her to see some Persian women. They were of high family and in purdah, so four or five doors had to be unbarred and opened before we got into the bright courtyard. At one end there was a wide verandah with an old vine growing heavily over it, and on a rug in the sun sat a group of Persian women and girls: the old grandmother, and her son's wife, and his son's wives – two girls of about fifteen and sixteen. They were all very courteous and serene. Slim and wide-eyed, they stood up when we arrived, and though I couldn't understand a word they said, we smiled at each other quite happily. The girls had straight black fringes under gold caps, which were wrapped round with stiff white gauze. They wore full white trousers and coats of blue and white striped silk. Their faces looked radiant – one possessed a baby boy, who clung to her gauzy veil, hiding his face in it. Adorable little creature, with his round embroidered cap and small coat of grape-coloured velvet. In his fat hand he gripped a jade bracelet he had pulled off her arm. There was hardly any furniture in the house – practically nothing but a low table with a threadbare silk rug thrown over it, and a pan of charcoal burning. It all seemed very peaceful and poetic to me, and I half envied them their seclusion.

Coming through the Bazaar that evening, each shop seemed a separate work of art set in its own frame. In front of the fruit-seller, the grain-seller, in front of the shops for velvet waistcoats, and the dyers with their huge cauldrons simmering in front, were put jars of vermilion tulips – sometimes a row of bunches of red tulips. Glowing beauty of men and flowers! You look so alive and fierce-feeling, you men in skins and velvet! – it seems a good symbol of you, that scarlet, arrogant tulip.

Not many weeks later everything was parched and hot, and then suddenly, one afternoon, there was a storm – a rain-storm, thunder-storm, dust-storm and sand-storm – all in one. Great clouds of dust circled up into the air and thunder rolled in the middle of the murk of flying sand; darker it grew and darker; and then, all at once, there was a turbulent muddy river streaming across the desert from the hills. In the evening the rain stopped, the air was moist and cool, and how washed and wet all the roads looked.

We went down to the Fruit Market. There were purple clouds piled up behind the mountains, and only a few rays of stormy sunshine broke through. The covered market was full of yellow and green melons, some of which were split, showing the rosy flesh inside; men were sitting in a circle amongst them, talking and eating; on one side was a group of huge fat-tailed sheep. The last rays of the sun fell on the piled-up fruit, the huge sheep, and the men in their rough yellow

[37]

skin jackets. One of the sheep near me had an orange cross marked on its back, and a necklet of forget-me-not blue beads shone in the white woolliness of its neck. It was eating a yellow melon and a boy was feeding some others with the split pink bits. I stood still – not thinking – soaked in the stormy and gorgeous colour of it all – gazing at the masses of rounded fruits and feeling the rough vigour of the Baluchis and Pathans as they strode about the market. Then all at once my eyes fell on another (a very different) figure, just as big and vigorous, it is true, but so different, and there, to my surprise, was a man who had been on the ship with us – a Canadian. He too had just seen me, and after a moment he came up in his rather lumbering, awkward way and said he guessed travelling on the same ship was good enough for an introduction out here. I answered, laughing, that I guessed it was, and added that since then I had come across one of his books. He was staying in the place for a few weeks more, he said, in order to study the various tribes scattered about in the district.

During the next three weeks I saw quite as much of him as I wanted. For I didn't really like him. To begin with he was heavy and clumsy to look at, no movement of his had any precision or grace, and then he was heavy and clumsy, too, in mind. But he did have some power, and I couldn't ignore it. I met him at dinners and dances, or at the Club if we went there. He used to talk and talk, and I couldn't help listening. Perhaps it was only my imagination that made me think he was trying to get some hold over my mind, and that I was trying to escape. When he was sitting there, with his brooding look upon me, and I listened to his oddly penetrating talk, I felt it wanted a real effort on my part to shake free again. I don't know what he asked of me quite; probably not much, but I was afraid of being disturbed in the world of my own imagination and of being taken into the other stranger world of his mind. He asked me later on why I had avoided him on board; he had watched me and wanted to talk to me, he said, because, forsooth, my 'face was so luminous!' And now he wanted to come for walks with me because with me 'things appeared fresh' to him.

Ungainly he was, and uneasy, but he had dignity. He gave me the impression of standing completely by himself in life. He didn't belong to any particular class, and in this country where everybody has his place he seemed extraordinarily independent and detached.

The thing I most enjoyed while his presence hung over me was the native horse show and races; and perhaps what helped me to enjoy that was the thought that my companion was to leave on the evening of the same day. The show was quite an exciting one. The natives had put on their strength and donned their most beautiful garments; and never were a people who wore more satisfying clothes – broad stripes and checks and little rough coats, more rich in colour and design than any we are able to turn out.

There was a great crowd on the race-course – Pathans, Hazaras, and people from Khandahar; a crowd of horses, children, women, many of them on asses, camels with decorated saddles, bullocks with crimson and blue saddle-cloths. Peaked caps, white trousers and velvet coats swarmed everywhere, and amongst them were English soldiers. Up in the poplar trees shone gold caps and the gold lace on coats; camels' heads peered over the thick crowd at the railing, and some of the men managed to get a view by standing on bullocks' backs as if they were tables.

The course was very indifferently kept; not only did wrestlers perform there but the native band (which had an encounter with the military band and vanquished it) sat in the middle of the grass, only moving when the race started, and going back again afterwards to finish its playing of 'Mahmoud of Ghazni' or 'Zokhmi Dil' (The Wounded Heart), on painted, twanging instruments. One of the most amusing events was a race for zemindars; they started as hard as ever they could, so as to make a good impression when going past the thick of the crowd, then eased down, and only put on pace again when they came back before a full audience. They rode without stirrups, nor did they wear jackets – but just big blue or olive green trousers and perhaps a crimson silk handkerchief tied round their dark heads. As they dashed along they waved their arms; their turbans, if they had any, flew out behind, and they shouted continuously. Then there was tent-pegging, followed by feats of horsemanship; slim Pathans stood up on galloping horses, jumping off and on again as they careered along. The camels that were competing had been ornamented with blue beads and quantities of red tassels. During the race the cushions and tassels fell off, and the rest of their decorations streamed out in the wind. Before the finish some of the camels left the course, disappearing altogether in spite of their frantic riders, while all the crowd yelled. Finally, as the sun set, most of the onlookers swarmed on to the course, spreading white cloths over the grass upon which they said their prayers.

We waited till the end. The Canadian stood by me while the rest of the party was collecting itself.

'I won't forget you,' he said. 'You don't much care to be with me; I know that. You see how well I understand.'

And I, looking into his grave face, knew that he was more of my own kind than anyone else there. He had not caught me, he did not hold me captive, but we could meet, as I then saw, in some region of the mind where the others did not enter.

'Well, you see,' I said at last, ' although I seem dreamy, I like gaiety – I like to be laughing. I don't want – other things.'

'Yes, you are rather frightened – and perhaps rather spoilt,' he answered, half smiling. 'But I should have left you what you are – a child.'

I met his gaze and knew he was right, and I suddenly felt terribly ashamed of my faintness of heart.

'Look at all those people,' he went on, 'going home by different roads, and praying. We all go different ways about the earth – and to heaven too. For, of course,' he added, 'religion is the only real thing anywhere.'

The sun was setting and down the dusty roads

[42]

the crowd streamed away – children on oxen, superb young men on horses with long tails, whole families, just bundles of red and brown and yellow, borne aloft on camels. The pointed hills, which had flushed to an unsubstantial apricot and peach colour, now paled again and were chill and slaty.

'Some time I'll write to you,' said the Canadian. 'Good-bye.'

We have now reached the month of May. All day the naked sun burns on till nearly eight in the evening. I went into the garden just now to see if there were ripe figs on the trees, but it was too hot to stay there. I must wait till sundown. It is better to sit indoors and gaze out through the vibrating air at the mountains that stand between us and the sea. Soon we shall go across the plain and beyond it, and this place will be no more than a series of pictures in my mind – vivid in patches, but with hardly any personal connection. For this land still remains alien to me – dramatically distant. Any one of these strange Asiatic faces, looked at deeply, sets one so far away.

Yesterday evening I went out to buy some Bagdad silk, and I felt that even the suffering I met upon the way could hardly touch me, so remote did it seem. But oh, the beauty of those narrow streets! Covered over for the sake of shade, they are rather dark, but how they glow with colour! In this season, before all the shops, instead of tulips, there are jars of tightly bunched pink roses – the chill pink rose of Persia. And some pots of geraniums. I walked slowly, for it was still very hot. One man, young and strong, was selling drinks, all of bright colours in glass bottles, and the stoppers to the bottles were made of magenta paper, sprayed out. Behind him hung an embroidered purple curtain, worked all over with little white flowers. His eyes were large and grey and he wore a dark blue turban, in the side of which was stuck a bunch of white roses. Cross-legged and serene he sat on the counter, with his thick curly hair falling over his shoulders and his row of nosegays in front. He sat there so quietly, and opposite him on the other side of the road was an old beggar woman crouching against a mud wall. Like Lazarus she was covered with sores, her dusty matted head was bent almost to the ground. She was grey with dust and dirt and there were no dogs to lick her sores. I gave her a little money and stood there vaguely looking at my crisp muslin dress against that heap of rags. The white dress, the white roses, the white embroidery

on the silk curtain, my scented soft handkerchief –
how fresh and sweet they all were! And how
helpless I was beside this misery! I glanced up the
shaded street, and the young man looked rather
scornfully at me. 'Only a beggar! – Only a
woman!' he seemed to say.– 'Your strength is no
good for this,' I answered, half out loud. 'If
only the young Christ could pass this way and she
could touch the hem of His garment!'

IV

THIS garden is a green gloom in a sandy plain;
outside its walls lies the sun-baked little town. I
am writing on a long verandah flecked with sunlight. Close in front of me, like a medieval Italian
design, convolvuluses are growing; they are
trained straight upwards round the wooden posts
of the verandah; among pale, heart-shaped leaves
their velvet-streaked, frail flowers – all opening
widely to the sun – are transparently, brilliantly
blue and purple and magenta. Beyond, far away,
are pointed mountains, faint in this fierce light.
We have come for a few days to the desert land on
the borders of Afghanistan and Persia. How
dreary these Eastern countries seem if one thinks
one has to stay in them for long! And can they
ever be intimate or homelike to anyone, these
barren Eastern houses? I wonder. But perhaps
this garden one could love – this garden with its
monster vines that shade curling paths, and all its
almond trees thick with green almonds, and its
dark-leaved quinces. I found a tortoise on a path
one evening, but it hissed at me when I touched
its horny back.

In one part of the garden convicts are at work.
They seem happy; anyhow, they laugh a good deal,

and it is only occasionally one hears the chink of
chains. This morning I watched them spading up
the hard soil; robust and vigorous they look,
pressing the spade down with strong feet shod in
pointed slippers. One of them has a waistcoat of
peach-coloured velvet embroidered with white,
another has a worn orange-coloured coat and a
scarlet cap, but most of them are in white from
head to foot and wear stiff gold caps from beneath
which their curly hair hangs down.

We had to come over a high mountain pass to
get here, and then through desert. At first it was
bare but not fantastic country; we met quantities of
flocks and herds that were being driven in from
the south – white and black sheep with their
lambs, goats and bleating kids, strings of camels
led by shaggy-looking men and women who
strode along gaunt-limbed and strong. Then, as
the country changed, I kept saying to myself that
this must be what the moon looks like or some
lifeless star, for the landscape had indeed a most
unearthly appearance – low ranges of arid hills
with strata of many-coloured rock set abruptly at
every angle, skeletons bare of flesh, their edges
sharp against the burning sky. Scattered about
were heaps of clay of every shape and hue; they
looked like gigantic anthills or growths of some

monstrous fungus. They gave the impression, too, of being poisonous, as though they had only a hard outer crust and were porous and rotten inside. What a fabulous look they gave to the scene! The pale green and pink and white mounds curling and spreading themselves about – a dwelling-place for slow dragons surely. The ground was baked hard; the fiery sky was like a blue tin lid laid over the earth, and there were no clouds to 'cool the cheek of the day'. As we rode through the hot little defiles the light seemed to make the rocks vibrate. By the time we were nearing the end of our journey I was very tired – too tired to look at the camels ploughing, or at the men clad in full white trousers and crimson waistcoats, who were working the dusty soil. Nothing could kindle my delight any longer – not even the faces and gilt caps of the running children, dressed like little princes and princesses, whom we met on the outskirts of the straggling town. I could do no more than stare vaguely before me as we rode down the long straight avenues of poplars with irises growing thickly beneath them. At last we came within sight of our destination. Far off we saw the high mud wall enclosing this garden, and the tops of the trees showing above the wall. How restful it was when we got there! The garden was

cut up by narrow paths winding among the
apricot and almond trees and leading to small
shady secret places. In the centre was a patch of
darker shade made by a cluster of mulberry trees.
The birds were singing loudly everywhere; the big
petals of the quince blossoms gleamed ivory white
in the dusk, and beyond along the far horizon
stretched the pale jagged mountains of Persia.

It was too hot and the glare was too great for
us to go out in the middle of the day, but the next
afternoon we were to pay a formal visit to the
Tribal Chief of the district who lived in a fort in
the middle of the town. Walking through the
narrow dusty streets I wondered if anywhere else
in the world were shops that glowed as splendidly
as the silk shops here. Their sudden splendour!
The sparseness and dryness of the colour outside
made all the more violent the richness of the piled
up silks within – the green like parrots' wings
seen in sunlight, the deep blue as of iris or gentian,
shades of pink and orange as vivid as nasturtium
petals. There were silks like a flame, silks of pure
rose colour, silks of magenta and gold and purple.
The man who kept the principal shop was a
refugee from Kabul. His lined thin face was half
smiling; he had criss-cross marks on his legs
where the red-hot irons had been laid when he was

in prison there. He showed us skins as well as silks; soft snow-leopard skins were lying about everywhere; he had, too, painted lutes and painted chests and boxes. His boy was in the dim back part of the shop, leaning against the bright rolls of silk. Dressed in a short coat of dull yellow leather, he stood there, apparently dreaming, and high on a shelf above him was a striped bottle in which had been stuck a bunch of polyanthus.

The fort was built, it seemed, of clay and stones. It had been swept and made clean for this visit, and the people had put on their finest clothes. We were taken through a courtyard to a tower, and then up some stairs to a bare, light room where the Chief was sitting waiting for us. He was an oldish man and burly, with a short curling black beard and a broad face. While the others talked about taxes and irrigation and fighting, I sat there silent. Before us was a table laden with melons, long white Kabuli grapes, apples from Kulu, and the sticky sweetmeats of the country. A few flowers in a tiny jar seemed to be aware of their own inconsequence just as I was. For I was the only woman there, and as the men went on talking I lost all heart and took no comfort even from the tea which was offered in gaily patterned Russian cups.

When this was over we climbed yet higher up

the tower of yellowish clay and looked down from
the roof over the country lying still in the faint
rosiness of the sunset light. All along the roads
were high hedges of loose pink roses. The dense
blue-green of the crops ended abruptly where the
water supply stopped. Long wavering lines of
camels trooped towards the town, looking just
the same colour as the sand they were treading on;
a bevy of women, swathed up like bundles in
their robes of weathered pink and red, rode in on
slow-moving oxen. It was beautiful – I knew it
was beautiful; but oh, the harshness of it! In my
faint-hearted mood I saw everywhere signs of
struggle and fight: no blade would grow here
without water laboured for under the blazing sun;
no sheep or goat could live here without the fear
of wolf or jackal; no traveller was safe from
robbers, no woman from man; no one could even
ride at his ease because of the rents and chasms
in the sun-baked ground. 'Yes, even the roses,' I
said to myself, 'are plucked and crushed, when at
their freshest, for the scent they will yield. And
no trees anywhere except the trembling poplar!
How dreadful to live in a country without trees! –
O dear rich trees of England, standing about in
the soft fields for no reason except that you are
beautiful and beloved!'

It seemed from what I heard that the Chieftain
of the Province was a monster rather than a human
being. Cruel and treacherous, he lived in his
squalid palace above the low town, with a hoard
of treasure hidden in his cellars underneath. This
treasure, they said, was guarded by a swarm of
black snakes that lived in the darkness below.
The thought of that man filled me with a horror
of all this country. I hated him with his debased
face, his filed and pointed teeth, his diseased
palace-horses that were never taken out, his dirty
zoo of wild animals, cramped in small cages
against the hot palace wall. As I looked around
from the tower a sudden anguished longing and
love for England dimmed my eyes and veiled the
clear-cut view. I longed passionately for the
tender landscape of home, for the views continually changing under changeful skies, for the soft
falls of friendly rain, for the fragrance of summer
evenings. I thought of the air, breathing of the
honeysuckle that grows over the uneven hedges
and of the smell of lilac still dewy in the morning.
I thought of ash trees in the winter stillness,
shaped like branching coral; I remembered flat
elder blossoms spread motionless in the heat of
summer suns, and weeping-willows like green
rain, and rivers and water-weeds. I remembered

the smell of water-weeds, pulled dripping from their streams, the freshest, coolest scent of all. I remembered, too, drifts of damp fallen beech leaves – all these things became real to me in a moment on that tower so many thousand miles away.

V

THESE cantonments in northern India are all one colour, not the tawny colour of the desert but just dry dust-colour. Now, as I write in the hot hour before luncheon, there is a light dust-storm passing along outside, making the soft white road still softer and thicker with dust, and the dry trees with their rattling leaves more colourless still. Horsemen go along the road occasionally, and soldiers constantly; native cavalry have been passing by, and now in the middle of the dust-storm go the mule transport and one or two camels. The men are trying to keep the dust out of their eyes – the camels are never concerned with anything that happens, always bored and always half resentful.

I love this bit of life. I love my little white-washed room and the thick bunch of orange blossom on the dressing-table; I have a vase, too, full of the big lilac flower that looks like butterflies with their wings outspread.

How new it all is! Soldiering mixed with hunting is practically the whole life of those I am with now. Nearly every one rides – every one English that is to say, and every one seems to be the same sort of age. There are no old people here, and

scarcely any children, but there are crowds of
young men who are always ready to lend one
ponies, or to arrange rides on elephants, or drive
one home from the polo in their dog-carts. And
I – even I! – have become sporting. I hadn't been
here two days before I was made to hunt. My
brother Richard, whom I have now joined, had
got a pony for me; and still feeling slightly bewildered I started off with him before dawn for
that first day's meet.

It was in the cool starlight that we set out. We
crowded into a carriage with another girl and an
unknown man belonging to some native cavalry
regiment, who dozed in a corner. I looked out of
the window and felt the chill air and saw the stars
pale before the dawn; I thought of India stretching
away to the snows and to its tropic seas, and the
others began to sing sleepily songs that they had
heard at regimental concerts. After a while we
reached a bridge over a canal and saw a ring of
horses standing, and a ring of muffled syces
hunched round a fire that they had lighted on the
ground to keep warm by. We got out stiffly and
mounted; then voices were heard and we saw the
shadowy hounds coming along the canal bank and
behind them more people riding. But how quickly
after dawn the day grew hot and glaring! We had

a long run that morning. We jumped endless
ditches and banks, and at last they killed the
jackal they were hunting, with its cowed and
pointed face. It looked so thin compared to the
hounds.

My pony, which had never been hunted before,
was quite untrained. At last it pulled and curveted
about so much that I got off, and Richard led it
and his own across the hot red plain, while I
walked beside him jumping the little ditches
clumsily in my long boots. How heavy my habit
seemed! How dusty and thick! My feet ached.
But India was new enough to keep me very
excited. It was so strange to be walking through
Indian fields. To stretch out one's hand and pick
cotton glistening in woolly pods! I saw some
trees with heavy vultures clustered on them; vultures always look old and ragged, they always
droop; their every feather seems to sag, and their
nests are old and ragged, too. I saw, too, a striped
wild cat sitting tense on a wall. Eventually, we
met our syces again outside the gates of an orange
garden where the air was flooded with the scent
of orange blossom. A milk-white bullock stood
there quietly, and a white-bearded old man,
covered with a yellow cloth, sat near it in the shade
of the trees thick with yellow-green fruit. He

gently replied, 'Salaam, Sahib,' when Richard said 'Salaam, Buddha' (old man), to him.

We bought some tangerines from a wayside seller who was squatting with a sulky face under the shadow of that high wall, his pile of sugar-cane and loose-skinned oranges in front of him. Then we hired a little cart, and so drove home, Richard slashing idly at passing bullock carts and sleepy drivers with his long whip.

On our verandah we found some of the others in Richard's regiment who had come to have breakfast with us. Everything was strange, including having breakfast with all those boisterous subalterns.

In the weeks that followed, Richard and I went out riding on most of the days that we didn't hunt. Early in the morning the Indian 'Boy' would come and wake me, putting a tray down by my side, and I, leaving it sleepily till the last moment, would jump up and dress when I heard the Boy come again to the door and knock. 'That master ready, missie,' he says. Then I hear the horses being led round outside, and catching up my long gloves and the little riding whip Richard had given me, I go out into the cool. We ride through the Gunners' stables with all the buckets set outside, and through the mud lines where the native women live. There are little clouds of dust where the Gunners are drilling; their khaki uniform is just the colour of the cantonment soil.

But I like best going to that square tank, dark and hidden with the mango trees around it; in the early morning there are generally some Brahmans doing their ceremonial washing there. One can see the sacred cord across their wet bodies. They scarcely glance at us, our worlds are, indeed, too far apart to merge, even for a moment, into one. A Fakir lives near by, too; he has a solitary little enclosure of his own, but he is not a bit gloomy nor abstracted; he is ready to laugh when Richard speaks to him. A dark red cloth is thrown over his strong shoulders, the thick hair falls round his fine rugged face; in those rough garments, perhaps John the Baptist looked like him.

In the evening all the English repair to the Club, where a band plays. We dance – the men in white flannels or polo kit and the women in habits or tennis clothes. At one end stands a refreshment bar where you get coffee and little plates of potato chips and grain called gram. After playing polo, the men come in, and after riding one stops there. A crowd is always standing on the broad steps in front, talking, smoking, listening to the band, while the crows flap about among the trees on the grass maidan in front, and the syces wait squatting by the dog-carts or horses, while the darkness falls.

And then came the evening when I saw Jack ride up. Hardly waiting for his man to run and take his pony, he walked straight in. The confused sound of dancing, the band playing and noisy talking, made an intricate pattern through which I heard his odd hard voice – curiously distinct – saying to some one that he had just come down from Simla. Richard was already dancing heavily in his riding boots. Some one brought me a cup of coffee. I felt suddenly tired. I knew that now Jack would try and draw me out of my own world of imagination. He came and stood in front of me, half smiling, but saying nothing. The lilting tune swung on; the couples passing and repassing on the shining floor made me feel dazed. 'Come,' he said. I shook my head. 'But of course, you're going to dance – you're going to dance with me.'

Richard was playing polo the next day, so Jack came for me in his car and we packed a tea-basket and drove off by ourselves. He was a little changed, his face burnt brown by the Indian sun; but his jerky voice woke the old thrill. We drove over the shaking bridge of boats; the river was so low that only two boats of the long line floated. Buffaloes stood knee-deep in the mud along the bank, mud-coloured creatures standing torpid, motionless in the sun. Then we turned down a palm-bordered track with the green crops of the Punjab stretching away on every side. We hardly met anyone on the way – only an old man carrying his hookah, and a dimpled little boy holding a stick followed by a herd of goats and brown sheep. With a laughing face, the boy led his flock along the track speckled by sun and shadow, and after him came a tinier boy, a naked gold-brown cherub, one rounded arm over the shaggy neck of an old goat, like a creature in some sylvan legend. We stopped near a group of trees that were full of parrots constantly flying out in a whirring cloud and then settling again. The green trees were thick with green wings and loud twitterings.

The car was left in the middle of the road – for there was no traffic here – and we unpacked our tea-basket, spreading the things on the grass in the shade. The spirit lamp leaked and the light flickering flame ran along the ground, burning up the shrivelled grass. Jack thought it would catch my old silk dress, but I wouldn't move – no movement seemed worth while, sitting there so peacefully in the warm afternoon. He lay on the ground smoking.

The magical evening light that is almost too rich, too spectacular, turned the thick half-grown wheat to prussian blue, and light veils of blue mist began to rise above the crops as the sun sank down. The dome of the great mosque far off stood clear against the sky that turned from gold to smoky Indian yellow. Quiet figures in dusty scarlet or dusty crimson moved homeward along the little field paths. It was time for us to go, too. Some lean sheep passing by, their poor fleeces gilded by the light, ate up the skins of our oranges. As I got up, the light breeze of evening blew my scarf over Jack's arm; he caught it and looked up, smiling. 'No, I'm not going to let go,' he said, 'I've got hold of a bit of you at last, flimsy though it be.'

We hardly spoke as we drove home in the cooling air. With Jack, who had been so much a part of home, I was more conscious than ever of the mysterious alien life around us. As we passed under the deep shade of the big banyan trees at the gateway of the Moghul garden, two sadhus were standing there, and for garments they had nothing but the thick ashes with which they were sprinkled. They had put down their begging-bowls and lighted a fire on the worn bit of ground under the trees. They stood and looked at us aloofly, leaning on their thick sticks. With hard, bony legs and matted hair, how unnatural those blue-grey bodies seemed; most sinister! My spirits sank as I looked at them. 'They despise us all, I suppose,' I thought as we went by; 'they certainly despise me, who am a woman.'

VI

RICHARD and Jack had been asked by a Maharajah whom they had met playing polo to come and stay with him for a day or two in the capital of his remote, sandy State. It was arranged that I should accompany them, and never shall I forget the long night and day journey to get there. The train window had to be kept shut, for the sand blew in and stifled us if the least crack was left open. So there was nothing for it but to do without air, and we lay panting on the leather seats through the melting heat of noonday. Thank heaven, we had oranges, pomegranates and Cape gooseberries to eat, and some figs in a little green basket made of fig leaves.

At last we arrived. An amiable man in Shantung silk and long ear-rings met us at the station. It was his duty, he said, to telephone to His Highness 'to inform him of our safe arrival'. This done, we drove down the sandy roads of the ochre-coloured city – long roads full of swaying camels, with groups of women at the crossways, going to the well before darkness came down. Farther on, in the streets and open places, were set big tables, polished and dark, and on them men sat cross-legged, smoking hookahs and talking.

They looked supremely comfortable, those circles of white-clothed bearded men sitting upon the tables.

On every side of the town the desert stretched away into lilac as far as one could see. Only a few scrubby trees and bushes of spiky camel-thorn grew there, and everywhere the clumsy wild pigs routed snuffling about with coarse manes growing half-way down their backs. Nothing in the desert but wild pig and sand-grouse, I was told; yet one morning early I did see a tiny deer bounding over the parched red earth.

The next afternoon we drove to the polo ground, which was all of sand too. One saw the dust in clouds and the whirling ponies in the middle of it. Richard, who was playing, found it very difficult to see the ball with all the flying sand, but he played as violently as ever, his sun-hat on the back of his head, his face very red, his white shirt fluttering. I thrilled with excitement as the players thundered past, the turbans of the Nobles streaming out behind, whilst they shouted in Hindustani or, more often, in English.

The Maharajah was very fond of his white Arab ponies, which had white saddles; between each chukker he gave them a handful of grass and came and praised them to us in his charming voice.

A band in the yellow uniform of the State played
at intervals, and after the game was over a man
came round distributing tight formal bunches of
flowers. Out on that dusty ground how fresh
those flowers smelt!

That evening we were to dine at the Palace.
Dressed up in our best, we drove off by moonlight
in a large barouche painted with an enormous
coat-of-arms. Two men sat before us in front and
two more stood behind. After passing through
the high outer gates we drew up before the huge
front of the Palace with its flag flying above it.
An Englishman in white uniform met us on the
steps and led us through a hall of yellow marble
out into a courtyard open to the sky. There we
waited until at last, when I was almost dazed by
the silvery whiteness of the moon shining on the
smooth white walls, the young Maharajah appeared, himself all in white, against the darkness
of a black archway. With us at dinner there were
some of his cousins – slim, lithe young men with
straight features. They wore gorgeous tight-
fitting coats, and their gallant air made the scene
look like one out of a fairy-tale. Men in vermilion livery waited upon us. It took three of
them to hand round all the trays of ingredients for
the curry. Our surprise as tray followed tray

amused the Maharajah, who advised us what to
take and what to avoid, some of the mixtures
being so very hot. While he talked to me about
England and about polo at Hurlingham, Richard
and his neighbour became very animated and
friendly over pig-sticking.

When the meal was over I was taken along
many corridors and up a flight of stairs to the
apartments of the Maharanee. The men, of course,
remained below, so we were without an inter-
preter, and as neither knew the other's language
we could do little more than smile at each other.
We did a great deal of smiling in the course of
that little call. The Maharanee's plump face was
young and mild, with blackened eyes and heavy
ear-rings. She wore a peach-coloured sari worked
with silk and an imposing necklace of uncut
emeralds and pearls. A musical-box was turned on
for my entertainment, and then a stuffed canary
was made to twitter mechanically in a gilt cage.
Before I went away some rather moist sweetmeats
and a syrupy beverage were handed round by a
fat woman hung with jewels. I didn't care much
about their amusements nor their sweetmeats,
but I did envy them their clothes, and longed
to be dressed in that Indian dress of rich modest
grace. I envied them their beautiful tradition

of clothes that goes on century after century unchanged.

When I came down again to join the others, the Maharajah asked if we would care to go up on to the high roof-terrace and look down on the country round about instead of playing bridge. So we mounted the broad steps, pale beneath the moon. The town, which had a rather savage aspect by day, lay far below us, austere and calm. Nothing stirred anywhere. Sharp and clear in the bright light were the pallid houses, with wooden camel saddles hanging up by their doors; the flat roofs and thick mud walls broken by black shafts of black shadow.

I walked across the roof to look out over the other side, and on the ledge of the balustrade there lay a young dove, dead, with tiny clenched feet. I looked wonderingly at the utter quietness of it, the soft neck lying back, the peaceful head on one side – like a child asleep – the bright eyes closed, all so relaxed, so soft-feathered. When I turned again the men were leaning against the trellised wall, smoking and laughing over some joke. With the deep far blue of the sky beyond them how amazingly vital they looked! Supple figures in shot green and gold, in pale shimmering blue and white, and on their heads high turbans of crimson and turqouise. The moonlight glittered upon them; and there too were Richard and Jack, distinct in their severe evening clothes; the Maharajah had his hand on Jack's shoulder and they were all talking eagerly. My mind went back to the dove, and it seemed impossible to me that any of those active living shapes should ever grow old or die.

A Hindu feast was observed the next day, the ceremony consisting in carrying a goddess to a distant well and there worshipping her; but none except Hindus would be allowed to come near. Our host, who was taking part in the ritual, sent one of his A.D.C.'s to look after us and take us to the Fort, from which we were to see the procession start. Within the walls lived the aunts and great-aunts and women relations of the reigning Prince, with two hundred more women to wait on them and bring them the gossip of the bazaars. The A.D.C. looked very smart in white muslin, with shining long boots and spurs and a rainbow turban, the long ends of which hung down his back. A little cane in his hand, he walked lightly along, leading us to the terrace from which we looked down into courtyards and arcades. The sweltering courtyards were already crowded with women, their necks, arms and feet weighted thickly with bracelets and jewels, besides which they wore nose-rings, toe-rings and ear-rings in abundance. More and more densely did the people press and crowd in, perching themselves like flaming birds on the walls, on the roofs, and on the polished bronze cannons.

Very soon the different regiments marched up with flying pennons and passed with the band into the main courtyard, where the Maharajah's elephant was waiting, its shadow huge against the whitewashed wall. Then down the empty road from the Palace there came a light green car. It was the Maharajah, and with him was his wife, hidden behind silken curtains. But there was still some time to wait before the procession made a start and began to wind through the gateway below us. First came the soldiers, led by their band, then a bevy of rather coarse-looking dancing girls. These were followed by men beating great gongs slung from their shoulders, and they beat them with such vehemence that the din, harsh like the naked glare, was absolutely stupefying. And now came the goddess. She was carried high in the middle of a horde of singing women with covered faces – a grotesque little figure hung with garlands. All around her, like bees, the women

[69]

swarmed – in ruby and magenta, rose, striped orange and gold. Behind the goddess came the Maharajah and his little boy, riding a massive elephant. They sat on golden seats shaped like birds; the elephant was hung with supple cloth of silver which shimmered and shone in the sun. Its head was adorned with stiff aigrettes of emerald and crystal, and its ropes were crimson and red. The Maharajah and his son were dressed alike in soft white; the light flashed on the diamond ornament fastened in front of his big turban and on the smaller ornament of his boy.

They came slowly through the high gateway and all the people pressed round salaaming and shouting, 'Rao Sahib! Rao Sahib!' As he passed, he looked up at us and waved his hand and smiled. Behind his elephant came another, also caparisoned in silver, with a rider in turquoise satin and pearls. And then followed the tail of the procession – dancing horses with harness and head-pieces of real gold and golden bells hanging nearly to the ground; they were gravely led along by tall men in pure vermilion. Last came empty carts with canopies of velvet, for the goddess in case she tired. Upon the horns of the white, meek-headed bullocks that drew them were silver sheaths and on their backs trappings of silver that swung to their slow tread. Like a brilliant snake, the long line dragged itself down the dusty scorching road and disappeared at last into the desert.

Having watched it out of sight, we continued to sit there for a while. How peaceful this terrace was now; how delicious the silence after the shouting of the crowd and the tearing sound of the trumpets. The whole town was wrapped in silence; it seemed that scarcely anyone was left in it. Below me, in the shade, a dusty elephant was quietly shifting heavy balks of timber; presently a woman came out into a small enclosed garden and shrilly scolded a man who was working there. The man made no answer and she disappeared into the house again. At last we turned to go. Jack, who was anxious to understand the ritual of the feast, put a question to the A.D.C., who replied, smiling, that it would be very difficult to explain. Jack shrugged and said that the longer he stayed in India the less he could understand what we were doing in the country. 'But if it comes to that,' he added after a slight pause, 'what are we doing anywhere?' And the A.D.C., perhaps finding this yet more difficult to explain, replied, still smiling, that 'life was but a candle in the wind'.

VII

I WALKED rather timidly along the causeway to where the Temple shone golden and fabulous in the middle of the tank. The coral dawn had already faded, but it was still early in the morning and the tranquil water looked like dull steel. Inside the Temple itself it was chill, but the moving sunlight was just beginning to strike through the open sides and arcades and touch the shining walls; it fell too on the yellow flower-offerings tossed up into a soft mound in the middle.

Pigeons flew about, outside and in; on the ground sat a man swathed in dull blue, just the colour of the pigeons, and their burnished metallic wings were matched by the steel daggers stuck through his blue turban. He sat there, his face expressionless and as motionless as a mask, his eyes fixed in a trance so deep that it seemed as though they could never move again. I gazed at him, keeping almost as quiet as he, and feeling almost as deeply entranced – so still was he in his blue clothes backed by the golden walls and the golden heap of blossoms, while the blue pigeons fluttered full of movement round him.

Some old musicians sat cross-legged on the floor, making a music that had no end. Occasionally they would burst into a hoarse untidy singing; the singing grew louder, grew fiercer, grew almost frantic, before it suddenly quavered out and the music fell back into its old quietness. What was the meaning of this sudden exultation that bubbled up out of their torpidity? It excited one by its vehement, inexplicable spontaneousness.

Men and women in silks and gauzes began to wander in and out, presenting offerings to the priests, touching the ground with their heads, and doing their ceremonial washing.

And now the whole Temple is swimming in golden light, and we go out and saunter along the marble terraces that run all round the water. Along the broad walks are white figures ranged against the white walls. These are holy men, murmuring blessings on water brought by those who pass by. There are also teachers passively droning or singing in a seemingly half-conscious state, whilst their followers squat round them in rapt attention. Others sit silent, either looking about or vaguely pondering.

Propped up against a pillar and almost lost in the folds of his salmon-coloured robe, there is an aged man whose eyes show that he has wandered far into some strange world of his own. Near him drowses a baby, huddled up on a heap of rose petals. It is dressed in a tiny coat of sapphire velvet; an embroidered cap, its only other garment, lies on the marble pavement near by.

One of the men with a calm and intelligent face has attracted a large group by persistently tapping a nail against a glass bottle. It is difficult to understand why the people stand watching and waiting without a sign of impatience while the small sound of the tapping goes on and on without end. But it is all so difficult to understand; at last one ceases to wonder, and a mood of acceptance descends over one. In this dream-like place all our ideas of energy and purpose are dissolved into meaninglessness; even Time is dissolved into the ghost of an idea and the Sadhus gathered here are as creatures outside time – as creatures in a state of being that is hardly rippled into life, like the water in the steady tank.

But Richard, who was bored, said he was sure no enlightenment would ever come to him in that way, and asked Jack if he had ever seen a holy man who really looked holy. Jack was silent for a minute, and then he said that once, on his way down from the Hills, he had met a fakir who was travelling to the mountains by measuring his length on the ground all the way up those steep and stony roads. From far off he had watched his slow progress through the lonely country and when he had come near and seen the man's face he was amazed, so peaceful and strong was it, and full of joy.

After a while we moved away; we went into the courtyard behind the Temple, and here everything was different. Here life was fevered and had a nightmare quality. There was a crowd of pilgrims in this place, the smell of the marigolds on the shrines was strong and rank in the air, no breath of wind stirred the heavy atmosphere, and every moment the sun grew hotter and hotter. Wreaths of jasmine, offered for sale in flat baskets, breathed out a dying sweetness; the garlands which had been given to us in the Temple hung round our necks limp and dead. I noticed the people looking at us with curiosity and felt that a current of hostility was running through them.

This was the resort of the Fakirs. Here were the Fakirs of travellers' tales – mis-shapen and fanatical men. One had apparently taken a vow not to comb or cut his hair, which, matted thick and high above his head, fell over his eyes which peered through with a feverish glare. Another was leaning against a corner of the wall, and him I imagined to be really mad. He stood there with hardly a wisp of clothing, shouting, and lifting

[75]

imploring but not unhappy hands. Not far from him another being – nothing but a bag of bones – crouched over a red charcoal fire, while the cruel sun beat down upon his back and head.

My eyes fell next upon a figure seated on the ground with one arm held stiffly upwards. It had been in that position for so long that it had withered and become unbendable. Jack stood in front of the rigid, unnatural creature. I could see the pity in even his aloof regard as he looked at the poor emaciated face. He put some money into the begging bowl by the man and turned away, saying that it seemed an odd road to lead to Heaven.

But we had not yet seen the most grotesque object in the place, the spectacle that attracted the thickest crowd. This was an ash-smeared figure in a tow-coloured wig who lay upon a bed of blunt nails. As he looked round from time to time, I noticed that his face, which was singularly coarse and meaningless, wore a look of great self-satisfaction; and when he saw us among his admirers he was evidently seized with the desire to make himself still more impressive. He fumbled for some time with one hand in a little tin box by the side of his spiky bed. We wondered what could be coming next, and some amongst the crowd apparently knew, for they watched our faces to see the impression made. So long was the interval of preparation that I began to think that nothing more would happen after all; but after a further pause, the man put on, with infinite solemnity, a pair of gold pince-nez and looked round with unconcealed triumph. No one smiled. We stared as if awed, and indeed we were almost awed; for could anything more fantastic have been done? There he lay proudly on his nails, clothed only in ashes, a pale wig, and pince-nez that glittered in the sun.

VIII

I STOOD leaning against a marble pillar in the shade, gazing idly at the small square garden on the roof of another remote palace. The marble was cool to touch. The arcade, with its white columns, gave shade to all round the little green space; but in the middle the oleanders and pomegranate bushes lifted their creamy and scarlet blossoms to the full heat of noon.

Opposite me two or three turbaned men were lounging in the sunlight. How beautiful they were, against the pale marble background, in their clothes of lilac and amber and faded vermilion. A weight of heat, a brooding stillness, filled the gigantic white palace with a heavy peace.

It was two hours since we had drawn up before the great towered gateway. For two hours Jack and I had followed the others about, rather absently, like children at a show. And now I was tired and stupefied by the heat, like every one else – excepting Jack, who walked restlessly up and down, smoking cigarettes as usual.

We had been first of all into the dusk of the Armoury, a dim place with a high painted ceiling and thin Persian rugs on the stone floor. A row of men, sitting along one side of the room, were making sheaths for swords. The new velvet sheaths, embroidered in gold, lay freshly finished upon the ground; the old ones, frayed purple and tattered scarlet, lay piled up in one corner. In another corner were stacked long painted sticks of gorgeous colours. Hanging on the walls were curved swords and spears that caught the light. Jack lingered to handle the unsheathed weapons, fingering the sharpness of the old worn steel.

From the Armoury we went along shaded passages where scribes sat copying from ochre-coloured books. Their lined faces were bent downwards; they never looked up at us; their slender fingers went on with the fine writing.

We came out into a court that was filled with the sound of music, and, looking up, we saw a little group of musicians sitting on a balcony singing in the sun. They made a bright jumble of blue turbans and coats pale green and rose; the sunshine glittered on their silver bracelets and toe-rings and ear-rings. They accompanied themselves on long lutes and little drums, and vaguely, continuously, their singing rose and fell.

In the court there was perpetual movement. Men came out from dark doors and gateways leading horses with high-pointed saddles and bright bows tied round their legs.

We wandered on. We passed along endless colonnades; we went under endless porticoes where guards, in their old discoloured uniforms, sat torpid along the marble seats, their curved swords laid on the ground beside them. We climbed flight upon flight of age-worn, yellowing stairs, and looking out through the carved tracery of the windows we saw beneath us, far below, the sunny town with its temples, and the lake, a sheet of turquoise, shimmering in the heat.

As the sun mounted the world grew more and more still. Every one seemed to be asleep. Only, far down, on the great terrace – wide enough for the parade of the Maharajah's whole army, elephants and all – a 'dancing-horse,' with a pink velvet cloth thrown over it, was being led up and down. It pranced, and the man in scarlet hung on to the jingling reins; the silver pieces sewn on to its cloth flashed in the sun; the black prancing shadow of it was sharp upon the ground. It was there for the Maharanee to look at from her windows.

And now Jack and I had reached the somnolent little green world on the roof. Jasmine was climbing up one of the columns, and I said to him that I must have a bunch of it, for jasmine and orange blossom were the two scents I loved best

[80]

in India. 'Jasmine is an emblem of sorrow. You had better choose orange blossom,' he answered, smiling. But I said that, like Nur Mahal, I had a passion for this Indian jasmine. 'It is entwined all up the walls of her tomb at the Taj,' I added. 'Do you remember? And in the Palace at Agra there are niches in the walls for vases which used to be filled with it.'

He didn't answer; and I went on talking about the Queen's rooms at Agra; of how from the windows one could look out and see the Jumna flowing wide and calm in the cool dawn, and the grey cranes standing on the banks as quiet as the palms; and in the curve of the river lies the Taj, with its domes floating like milky bubbles above it under the rose-flushed sky. I described the forest of slim pillars in the palace, with creepers of jade and lapis lazuli winding up them – rooms all ivory, set with fragments of onyx and agate – rooms with roses and lilies and irises eternally blooming upon their pale walls.

'If you met some one like Shah Jehan who could give you jasmine whose blossoms were mother-of-pearl and the leaves jade, perhaps then you would be ready to marry?' he said. And he went on: 'It is always the same. You are satisfied to look at the world through your eyes at a distance. You want no other–no *closer* reality.'

I had no answer. He was unhappy – and so was I, really. We left the roof terrace; we went down the innumerable stairs, and went out of the sleepy palace into the thronging streets. As we were driving along we met a wedding procession. First came the band, harsh and crude, followed by dancing girls singing with brassy voices, their full skirts stuck with gold tinsel; their bracelets and garlands and necklaces made up a jangling whirl as they circled and swung around. The slow horses following were almost hidden beneath brass and silver hangings; in the carriages sat children, stiff with silver cloth and stamped velvet. And then came a colossal elephant, an elephant painted in a formal design of squares, tapestry-green and blue. High on its towering bulk the bridegroom, a little tired boy, sat propped up half asleep, in a tight coat of cloth of gold. His eyes were thickly blackened, his head had sunk forward, the golden tassels of his festal cap fell dangling in front of his brown, babyish face; but he was too tired to care. His attendants waved fans over him; men walking by the elephant carried heart-shaped fans of velvet and peacocks' feathers which they swung to and fro;

the crowd gabbled and jostled about him; but he slept on.

In the cool of the evening we had tea in a garden enclosed by trellised walls, where the fresh leaves were very green. On the grass, in sun and shadow, moved peacocks, sapphire and emerald, a glowing troop. Not far off a great cupola rose against the yellowing sky, and in the trees around us the soft, grey monkeys were leaping.

At the far end of the garden, beyond the wall, there was a marshy lake. And as the sun was setting behind the stark hills and the desolate sand, two bare-limbed men stood by the water's edge in the fierce tawny light. They had bits of raw meat tied on to the end of long ropes. These they threw out as far as they could into the lake, following the flight with wild shouts that went echoing over the turgid water. And at once the stagnant surface was cut on all sides by big mud-coloured heads, and crocodiles came pushing themselves up the bank with their long mouths wide open. How I hated the yellow saw-like mouths and yellow teeth and dragging bodies.

While we were watching a roar shook the darkening air. There, in front of a cage built against a wall, more raw meat was being hacked up. Kites whirled round in the hot sky, swooping down now and again with an arrogant air and carrying bits of the tattered flesh away. Coming nearer, we saw a dusty tiger crouching in a corner of the cage, its flanks sunken in, and swishing its tail from side to side. It had just been trapped in a pit near by. Its yellow eyes burned so hotly that I feared to look at them. The Indian who was with us swaggered up to the cage and drew his hand insolently along it. Instantly the tiger hurled itself forward against the bars, which shook and rattled at its weight. It beat and beat again at the iron with its paws, opening its furious mouth. Such fierce, such maddened roars poured forth they seemed to tear one's ears and one's heart. There was a sick, almost shamed look upon Jack's face.

Then the tiger began to pace forlornly up and down and the floor of the cage was spattered with blood that came from a deep cut in its foot. We moved away, and I said to myself in a kind of angry revolt: 'Jack has to live in this country – and perhaps he can do something here. But what am I here for? I am not made for this.' And then, suddenly I felt far away. I couldn't recognize myself as the person walking by Jack's side. I was really walking in the soft fields at home – soft wet fields with fragrant feathery hedges.

IX

WE were back in the cantonments; four weeks
more went by, and then we moved into the city.
It was my last day before going up into the hills.
All through the warm afternoon I lay on the long
wicker-chair in the high whitewashed hotel room,
with the packed boxes round me and the bedding
all rolled up. Oh, that bare land! I have listened
for the last time to the yelping of the jackals at
night – that querulous whining bark that rises and
dies away so strangely. No more shall I hear the
Last Post in the distance, mounting through pain,
almost despair, to triumph at its close. The unknown was too close about one there; too keenly
one felt the earth driving on through unknown
spaces. When the unfamiliar stars blazed out in the
evening I was desolate with fear. In a sort of
panic I would repeat –

'Be kind to our darkness, O Fashioner dwelling in light
   And feeding the lamps of the sky;
Look down upon this one and let it be sweet
   In Thy sight, I pray Thee, to-night –
For this is a world full of sorrow,
For this is a world where we die.'

Light and amusing the life here seemed at first;
but as the heat became intenser other things be-

came intenser too – especially that poignant feeling of hazard and mortality. Life there was such a very chance affair. One of our friends, one of the youngest and most light-hearted, was at dinner with us one evening and died the next day.

For me, underneath the fun, there was a curious strain in the life which grew stronger every day. I didn't know how to order my thoughts, or how to choose which way I should go. Here Jack's face looked more reckless than ever, and my mind was troubled, confused and full of pain.

That last afternoon, when we went over to the cantonments for the last time, the pain of the place reached its height. We were to watch the Brigade Sports. When we got to the ground Jack came to meet us, and he stayed with me all the time. We sat side by side, hardly speaking – he, leaning back in his chair, his legs stretched out, his hat tilted over his eyes, the picture of dejection and utterly bored with the sports. In a dream I saw the men racing with white wet faces, and in between whiles soldiers dressed up as clowns performing antics under the blistering sun. Some men fainted after the obstacle race and fell into the arms of their friends. In a dream I saw the officers riding mules bareback, grotesque in fancy dress. The scarlet coats of the bandsmen seemed heavy with heat;

the band blared on in the exhausted air. All the time the same torturing questions were going round and round in my mind. Everything seemed to be crying out: 'You are alien here!' Although Jack said he hated India, he loved it too. There was something harsh and fatalistic in the secret country of his mind that was matched by the India around him.

The men had been running the quarter mile; their faces looked thin and pinched, their hair was wet on their foreheads. The ground felt like a stove. I heard Jack say: 'Would you hate the life very much if you stayed here?' And 'Couldn't you ever like it?' he asked again.

The intensity of the glare and his urgent questioning made everything seem taut and about to break up. There were the men's strained faces racing, the tight tape at the winning-post, that voice near me sharply edged with pain, and over all the aching sky with no cloud to soften it. My hands were stiff holding my flouncy parasol and I felt fixed and unable to move.

'Couldn't you ever like it?' he said again, so low that I could hardly hear.

The race was over, the tension broke. The soldiers began cheering, the band started to play again. I looked at Jack, trying to smile. 'Come!'

he said abruptly; 'your face is as white as your dress. We have had enough of this.'

We got into his car and he drove off; and when he stopped again I realized that we were under the walls of the old Moghul Fort. We walked along the quiet green ditch under those stupendous walls. There was no one there – only green parrots flying over our heads with eager pointed wings. We climbed up and up, high on to one of the crumbling walls, and sat looking down on a bare strip of ground, beyond which was the walled city. It was a Mohammedan holiday and the people were flying kites. From all parts of the city kites rose into the luminous evening air. Curved like shells, shaped like hearts and diamonds, they were poised in the light of the setting sun, pale, dreamlike, transparent. The children playing on the burnt-up grass beneath us shone like jewels, for they had on their festal clothes, and the little caps and shoes embroidered with gold thread glistened.

We sat watching. Along the broad worn road men and women, donkeys and beggars passed. All the men and boys were flying kites. Remote from life we felt. Our own lives were a dream, like everything else. Hushed sounds from the town were borne up to us. I watched a man sitting on a roof gazing up at his kite; he was as motionless as we were. A boy down below had a big kite of white and crimson, but he couldn't make it fly. We watched him run up and down the path again and again, but the kite would not rise.

The sky was now so bright that it became almost frightening; burning sequences of colour surged up from the west and all the blue above had turned sea-green. Then, suddenly from the grass ditch below, there appeared a black kite, diamond-shaped. It rose with grace – rich, dark, beautiful. It soared straight up into the wonderful sky. I cried out at the beauty of it. 'That is mine!' I said. And still it soared steadily up, right into the fire of the sunset. Jack followed it with his eyes, smiling rather bitterly. 'Very well! That is yours! And now, which is mine? I must see.' Looking round, he fixed his eyes upon a kite shaped like a scarlet heart. With a laugh he pointed to it. It was fluttering lamely near the ground, too heavy to rise.

A few hours later we were all in the train. The swift Indian night had come. We were to travel together till midnight; then our party would change into another train and Jack would go on by himself. Hour after hour I sat looking out of the window. The parched hot breath of the wind blew in, but made nothing cooler. The moon rose, golden and ample, over the stark hills. It shone on the little huts and palms; on fires built outside village walls, with rings of men sitting round the fiery glow which lit their dark faces and high turbans; on pools and dried-up river beds. It seemed to me that night as though each separate thing became significant of that land – the sight of a man sweeping with a bunch of peacock's feathers – the sight of a man in yellow strolling along a platform garlanded with pink roses.

At last we drew into our station. Crowds of people thronged it inside and out. They were sitting everywhere, on the hard ground, in clusters and circles, under the bright moonlight, their bundles and brass cooking pots beside them. A little apart, Jack and I gazed silently at the scene. The shadows of the roofs fell sharply on the white bareness of the earth; there was a dense blackness in the shade of the mud walls; beyond there stretched a cactus hedge; polished, it shone like blades of steel in that blue-white brightness. We seemed to be standing in a great silence – a silence so great that the bubbling chatter of the people scarcely disturbed it. All sound and all colour were quieted and chastened by the moonlight. While I was looking I had an experience which I had

had once or twice before in my life. That which seemed at one moment a chaos, a shifting kaleidoscope with no design, fell suddenly into perfect order, all its bits slipping into place. A new world opened out, a vast calm settled down on all the little scene, on us, on life. 'It is all one,' I said to myself. 'The plan – how clear! And how deep the unity!'

I turned, full of peace, to Jack and told him what I felt. 'Don't you, too, ever feel it?' I asked.

He shook his head. 'I see no order. I feel no plan,' he said in his hard voice. 'There's no sort of certitude in anything for me.' His words broke through my peculiar consciousness; the pattern fell to pieces again; the disjointed fragments drifted apart. And we were soon to part now. The night mail which he was to go by came thundering heavily in. We waited on the hot platform while the natives clambered into the crowded carriages, and chattered and screamed for the 'pani-wallah,' the man who carries water in a dripping goat-skin to all the thirsting hands and pots that are thrust through the train windows at every station, day or night.

In the tumult of noise we did not try to speak, and indeed there seemed nothing more for us to say. At last the train began to move and Jack

[91]

jumped up on to the step, and still he stood on the step as the train went out, with the red lights burning behind; in a few seconds he had slid away into the dark.

X

RICHARD and I rode our little ponies along a grassy path through the Himalayan forest. Our guide, Rigu, and some hill-men who looked after the ponies came behind. These men have the softest of voices, the very voices for these soft paths, and this soft air breathing warmth and freshness, and the green forest light. The head man looks like one of the Tudor kings and wears a square cap. Occasionally he brings me a handful of ferns and sweet-smelling roots he has collected. He laughs a great deal; Rigu tells us he is a good jester. There are ferns growing everywhere, and sometimes we see grey monkeys swinging from tree to tree.

Yesterday we loitered on the top of a hill where we were having a picnic and had to scramble down the steep slope in the gathering darkness back to our little forest path. The air was like wine. I could not help singing, and Richard, in the hope of stopping me, I suppose, kept on saying there were bears about. In the end it grew so dark that Rigu had to walk in front holding a white handkerchief out behind him to guide us.

We are on our way to stay with a Hill Rajah

in a little town in a fold of the lower ranges of the mountains. But the place where we slept last night is the place of all others where I should like to stay. As we arrived there in the dark, for the time being I could only see that it was a sort of Hansel and Gretchen wooden house that we were to sleep in. It was not till the morning that I realized what a delicious spot it was. It was so silent, so very sunny and smooth – all moss and fragrance and little streams, a warm grassy cup in the heart of the towering forest, and the great mountains rising around. As I stood on the wooden verandah and looked about, I saw tufts of smoke curling up from charcoal-burners' huts hidden among the pointed trees and the fresh scent of deodar logs was wafted across to me. 'The earth *is* sweet,' I said to myself, 'and who could want more than this?'

A little later some villagers came to us in the verandah and said there was a bear near by that had been spoiling their crops and stealing the little apricots from their trees. They wanted Richard to kill it. So in the afternoon he and I started out. Accompanied by Rigu and some others, we slid and clambered down the hill-side towards the place where the den was reported to be. Rigu, who led the party, was greatly excited. When we were near the spot I was told to climb up into a tree, and the hill-man whom we called Henry Tudor was to stay with me while Richard, Rigu and a few others stood behind some rocks a short way off. We had no idea from which side the bear would appear. As I waited, standing on a branch of a silver oak, I grew more and more nervous, and at last I shook all over. I could just see Richard in his rough khaki clothes, his collar open at the neck and his rifle in his hand. After about an hour of suspense something was seen sitrring amongst the trees and a deep thrill ran through us all. I could see Rigu peering over his rock, his curly head bobbing up and down with eagerness. Then my companion on the tree moved, touched me, and, pointing, said softly with intense excitement:

'Baloo! Baloo!'

I looked, and saw through the undergrowth a big soft black bear that stood on its hind legs and shook the trees, and then dropped down again noiselessly, and moved its great self about with extraordinary quietness.

'Baloo! Baloo!' my companion whispered: and at last Rigu saw him, and then Richard, and he fired. How loud sounded the noise that broke that stillness – and then the sudden plunge and roar of the bear as it hurled itself towards us! But while it was still a little distance off Richard fired again. There was another roar and a rattle of stones, and then silence.

Rigu jumped up on to a rock and danced there, waving his golden cap and shouting with joy, and I tried to climb down from the tree, trembling still, but no longer from fear; however, Henry Tudor stopped me, shaking his head and smiling and saying in his melodious tones something I couldn't understand.

The bear wasn't killed. He was badly wounded and had crept under some rocks. There was an interval while different plans were discussed. But it was already beginning to grow dark and soon the excitement died down, and thinking of the bear I felt wretched. With its furry coat it had looked so like a child's big toy. No more would it hunt about among the trees, hoping for honey.

We climbed slowly up the hill again. The villagers and their priest came and thanked Richard, salaaming again and again, and a man amongst them gave me a bunch of narcissi. How sweet the flowers were! And life, I thought, as I looked at the little group, what a mixed affair! Here the flowers and the delighted villagers, and there the wounded bear under the rocks in the dark.

FLOWERS AND ELEPHANTS

Next morning, after Richard had gone down and found and killed the bear, we climbed higher to go on with our journey. After riding some distance through green glooms the path brought us out on to the side of a hill, and there – through the straight rough trunks of gigantic deodars – I saw, with a soft inner shock, distant shapes, mightily ranged, the shining Himalayas. The sight struck me with a kind of terror, those mountains seemed wrought upon a different scale from anything else on earth or in the experience of human kind. 'And yet there are men living near those snows,' I thought, 'pilgrims, and holy men in caves, who have chosen that way of life.'

'Think of the hermits – the rishis living up there with their austere and solemn joys,' I said to Richard rather priggishly, pointing to the mountains with my riding-whip.

'Joys!' he laughed. 'Humph! What joys can there be up there in the cold? Neither joy nor use, to my mind.'

And he went on to ask me whether I thought *I* should find up there the peace they talked of; I told him I wasn't made of such heroic stuff and could not do without earthly delights, but that the rare people I was thinking of, who might belong to any race or any religion, existed on a different level and had a different sense of reality. But we didn't argue for long; he wouldn't agree that there were other joys – far more living and exultant – than ours.

After our midday meal we got out on to the open hot hill-side, harsh with wind and sun after the moist forest. We passed some bushes covered with small black medlars, which Richard and I ate with glee. There was a flock of goats on the brow of the hill. They had gathered themselves together in the shade of the one big tree there and a bright-eyed herdsman sat on a rock above them. The speckled sun and shadow fell on the scattered stones and goats all white and brown.

It must have been this that Shelley imagined when he wrote:

> 'Would he and I were far away
> Keeping flocks in Himalay.'

Our hill-men talked to the shepherd, who smiled and answered lazily.

Looking down and across the valley, we saw the town of Chahla lying pale in the sun, with a jade-coloured river flowing beneath its walls. It was a burning day. The ridged hills quivered in the heat; umber and pinkish hills made up all the

scene. The town is built on a steep slope; it is all
the same ochre colour, except the white palace
which sprawls above it. We rode on and down,
our ponies picking their way carefully among the
stones that went rattling down the steep path.
There were cliffs above the river with adventurous
walls running along the top of them, and a draw-
bridge had to be crossed before one could enter
the town.

Waiting for us at the end of the bridge was a
man who gave us the Rajah's card. The road then
leaves the turbulent river with the deodar logs
swirling down it and climbs in zigzags up the
opposite hill. We paused on a grassy space at the
top to rest our ponies, and looking back saw the
rough track by which we had come and the high
bridge over the river. Beneath us lay the State
prison; the prison-yard had two slender trees in
it and there the prisoners were sitting or sprawl-
ing in the sun. The thieves wear red caps, so
the native officials told us, the murderers blue.
Richard complimented him on the fine number of
murderers, and the man grinned.

We went on to the Guest House. It was a
spacious building set in a terraced garden running
along the top of the cliff, and the garden was full
of strange trees and flowers. The servants who

came out to meet us were dressed in green
and gold with a golden sun embroidered on
their turbans and on the front of their long
coats.

Our host, the Rajah, came to call in the evening. He was all in white and rode a black horse
with a man running at his stirrup. He had a thin
and rather sad-looking face and pale hands. His
family have been rulers here for hundreds of
years. He talked to Richard about international
politics, and of some articles about India in the
National Review; he also talked of the last Ameer of
Afghanistan and of Mr. Gladstone, who seemed a
queer couple to link together.

Before leaving, he turned to me and asked
whether I had seen and admired the view of the
snows on the way to this place. I said yes, and
asked him if he had ever known anyone who had
gone up into the high ranges as a hermit or on a
pilgrimage. He told me he had not; but his great-
uncle, who in his father's time had been Vizier
of the State, had suddenly given up everything
in order to become a 'religious'. No one knew
where he had gone; he had disappeared, leaving
all the world behind him.

After the Rajah had left I went up to my room,
and then out on to the balcony. It was now dark.

Beneath me lay the garden and the deep ravine, above were the glimmering snows. I thought of the Temple in the town which the Rajah had told us about where a service had been held every night since A.D. 600. There was no sound in the air but the hum of insects and the rush of the dark water flowing deep in its bed below. Up the pillars of the verandah jasmine, roses and stephanotis were twining, and the starry flowers gleamed white in the dimness. It was magical! The whole world seemed to be drugged with the perfume of the flowers and of the night. The sweetness of the scent troubled me; it drowned my disconnected thoughts, which melted into a dream of the soft damp forest, of the bear we had killed, of the prisoners in the bare yard, and of the pilgrims on their hard way. There was no moon; but the stars were blazing and by their light the snows were faintly seen. 'That other life,' I thought again, 'the life of search and prayer. . . .'

At last I turned to go in, and there, brushing against my face, was a full and perfect rose. Cream-coloured, it gleamed like a pearl in the still enchanted night. All romance, all earthly loveliness, seemed to lie folded in those lustrous petals. That rose at least was at peace within itself!

'Dear lovely life!' I cried out. 'Can the Yogis find anything more precious than this after all? This flower, this symbol, this promise that on the earth lovers shall "capture their eternal hour".'

XI

THE rain poured down on Agra, on the noisy
'choking streets, on the colossal rose-red fort that
seemed to sleep in its passive strength, on the
mosques and minarets, on the shimmering Taj
Mahal. It poured, too, with a deafening noise
upon our hotel. Such storm-rain as that hypno-
tizes one – I stood and watched and felt it in a
sort of trance – the water streaming off the roof,
the flowers beaten down, the clouds torn again
and again by swift blue lightning.

All the morning it had been intolerably hot; I
had wandered about my big room for hours trying to pack, continually sipping iced lemonade,
and standing between any window and door
where the tiniest draught moved. I had sat and
looked out at the trees from the balcony. They
were crowded with little parrots, tossing from
branch to branch restlessly, and two bright blue
jays sat perched on a dusty ledge. The red dust
blew chokingly about the yard outside where the
servants dozed in the shade. Then suddenly a
wind began to blow, but fiery hot; the parched
leaves fell pattering off the trees and the tawny
dust danced round and round in little columns.
Thunder rolled, and uneasily there fell heavy,

heavy drops on to the roof. There seemed a breathless pause before the eager rain came splashing down. Even the parrots' quarrelling had died away. How thick the rain fell! The dust became all at once red mud; the roads were little rivers with the drops falling deep into them.

We had planned to go to Fatephur Sikri, that derelict city which the Emperor Akbar built. He built it on a ridge in an immense plain, upon a spot where no one but the saint Salim Christi had lived until he founded his royal city, which after twenty-five years was utterly abandoned. It stands there still after these centuries; its mosques, its palaces, its Hall of Audience, its soaring pillars – perfect and stable.

The motor that was to take us stood waiting under the hotel porch; it looked rather stranded and absurd in a sea of mud. Vehemently the rain poured on. Everyone said it was too wet to go. A dead city, they said, was cheerless enough on a fine day, bats hanging from dank ceilings and snakes in the rubble of old walls; in the pelting rain and thunder it would be altogether too depressing.

'It is our last chance,' I repeated: 'I must go. I will go, even if I go alone.'

'What nonsense!' Richard exclaimed, and went

on to say that he couldn't understand why I was so 'crazy' over Akbar.

I said that it was better to be crazy about Akbar than about Napoleon. 'Napoleon,' I continued, 'makes a shoddy figure beside him – always boasting of conquest. Akbar said conquest by the sword wasn't worth calling conquest.'

'Napoleon was the greatest soldier that ever lived,' replied Richard.

'But Akbar was everything,' I went on; 'not only a soldier and Emperor, but a visionary and philosopher as well.'

'Oh, is that all?' said Richard.

'Not quite,' I answered, and told him that Akbar was also a wonderful horseman and musician – and a great hunter until his conscience forbade him to kill even the smallest of living creatures.

'Well, anyhow,' said Richard, 'I am not going to his city in this storm.'

Eventually a woman staying in the hotel declared that she was ready to accompany me, and we started off, feeling a little silly, under a mountain of rugs and waterproofs. It is twenty miles from the living city to the dead one – a strange desolate drive under the purple-clouded, sinister sky. We passed through a village drained of all living things except a few bedraggled dogs that barked at us as we went by. 'Is there a dead village,' I wondered, 'as well as a dead city?' But a little farther on we came upon all the villagers gathered in a field. They were surging together in a crowd, chanting loudly, and in their midst, from out of the green crops, a huge canary-coloured idol stood up erect and hideous. The people were singing and dancing round it; un-natural and grotesque swayed the erection which they sometimes seized and carried along. Like a large vacant toy it gazed blankly in whatever direction it was set down. How strangely light did the wet meaningless shape of blotched yellow and white stand out against the thick stormy sky.

Driving on down the broad road of Akbar's making we talked in a desultory way of the Moghul dynasty. I said it seemed odd that so little should be made of Akbar, who outshone all the most brilliant figures in history. He always thought of the whole, not of parts; his curiosity and energy would not let him rest in incomplete-ness. His life was an endless search. 'It is Thee I seek from temple to temple' was his constant thought. I said I would rather have seen him than any man who ever lived, excepting, perhaps, Saint Paul.

'A rather ugly little Jew, I expect,' my companion remarked. 'And with him we should have had to be content to be seen and not heard. He didn't like women who talked much.'

'I should have been more than content to listen,' I answered. 'And so, too, with Akbar. Besides, in his case the mere spectacle would have been wonderful enough; his pomp and ceremonial, his magnificent caprices—for instance, the games of chess with elephants and horses and wreathed children for pieces, moving about in the courtyard of black and white marble.'

We had come at last to the outer walls, the gateways and the ruined fortifications of the city. The motor stopped by a deserted doorway and we got out. The storm was still raging, but in the distance; here the rain had ceased and the gaunt red palaces stood up wet and clear against the dark sky. Forked lightning ran and flickered behind the minarets and domes, but in the superb city itself nothing stirred. We went forward. Feeling small and shy, we walked across a great emptiness of courtyards shining with pools of rain. We went down colonnades and cloisters – past towers and terraces and tombs. Oppressively royal did the place seem even now in its desertion.

I wonder if any other spot upon the earth is so

deeply stamped with the mark of a single man? Akbar's virility and imaginativeness are seen everywhere – in the small austere chamber where he spent his short night, in the Hall of Audience where he debated with wise men of every religion, in his Mosque, in his Hospital, and in the small but exquisite Palace which he built for Birbal, his minstrel friend.

Grass was now growing between the stones that pave the city, and nothing but the peacock's harsh cry of wet weather breaks the silence in which it lies. Having left my companion behind, I went on, moving quietly, half afraid of the sound of my own footsteps. Before me there rose the mother-of-pearl tomb erected for the Saint. Feeling muddy and damp, I stood looking at the shimmering shape, set like a pearl amongst the massive red walls, the dark wet paving-stones of the courtyard reflecting its milky sheen. It set me thinking of that deep reverence for holiness that is always found in India. 'But even this is not the heart of the place,' I thought, and moved on uncertainly. A small uneasy wind had sprung up; I was feeling tired; a peculiar melancholy lay over everything, and I wanted to turn back. And then all at once I got there! I had come upon the Gate of Victory – a gateway crowning a vast flight of steps that descends into the plain. There is no road beyond, only a great spread of desolate land. I stood at the top of the steps; the glorious portal rising above me lifted its towers and cupolas high into a grey sky of drifting tattered clouds. A broad band of white marble inlaid with black Persian characters runs round the huge red span of the arch, and I remembered the words which Akbar had there engraved:

'Said Jesus, on whom be peace: The world is a bridge. Pass over it, but build no house therein. Who hopes for an hour hopes for Eternity. Spend the hour in prayer. The rest is unknown.'

The damp air was soaked with quietness; below, smudged amongst the few trees were three little huts; the smoke of an evening fire trailed slowly up through the heavy atmosphere, and the smell of it came mingled with the poignant smell of wet earth. It was so still! yet less than four centuries ago this place had been full of brilliant life; men and women had poured jostling each other up and down the way where now only a peacock sat huddled on a wall. The plain, immense and forlorn, stretched away and away till the green crops faded into unsubstantial blue; India itself seemed to lie there before one. And those great steps, in

how sublime a fashion did they rise out of the
plain – so enduring, and no one to use them – so
magnificent, and no one to wonder!

A door at the base of one of the towers stood
open, and, going in, I found there was a twisting
staircase let in the wall. I climbed up it, the
crumbling plaster falling off in flakes as I went by,
and presently I came out on to a marble balcony,
which gleamed white after the rain. This was the
place where Akbar used to sit in the evening and
gaze out over his wide land. 'There were warm
showery evenings then, as now,' I thought, 'making places intimate and tender; and he must have
looked out upon a scene just like this.'

I stood still for a long time, drenched in utter
loneliness, thinking how 'age after age the tragic
empires rise'. I remembered that not many years
after his death Akbar's bones had been dug up
and burnt and the ashes scattered to the wind. A
chill wind blew round me now. Already the pur-
plish web of dusk was blotting the distance out.
It was time to leave. I waited a moment to watch
a wet mongoose run across the steps far below,
and then turned to go down the dark stairs again.
As I went down in that blank silence fear struck
me. I felt the past was merging with the present
and might suddenly become tangible. I might see

Akbar! When I got out into daylight again, I was trembling. The peacock, startled by my sudden appearance, fluttered clumsily off the wall with a grating cry. I fled away.

XII

INDIA, all its magnificence and solemnity, its vast complicated pattern of men and religions, lies behind me now. Here in Ceylon living seems much simpler – a sort of intimate child's play. Here all thought is relaxed.

This lovely river in front of me flows along broad and still between trees and rustling bamboos that, spraying high into the air, are like towering fountains of green; the slow paddy-boats float lazily down-stream, passing in and out of liquid green shadow and liquid green light. Their thatched roofs give them a home-like air. Children and kids play together among the big combs of plantains that hang heavily – yellow heaps on the yellowish straw. Men, naked except for a loincloth, sit in front and behind; they chant in a monotone; they chew betel-nut, their mouths are scarlet with the juice.

Yesterday evening I went down to the steps by the river; a paddy-boat was lying there with the men squatting idly about it. I looked along the shadowed river and imagined it flowing on, mile after mile, through the warm spicy land; and then, as I looked, there came walking slowly down it an elephant with its mahout, in ruby-coloured cap, upon its back. When it came nearer the men in the boat waved and called, and the elephant turned towards us and came lumbering through the water to the steps. It stood in the clear ripples there and played tricks like a child; it tossed the water from its waving trunk in jets and falling crystal circles; it lay down in the river, its side alone showing like a round grey rock; it trumpeted in the sunny stillness of the evening, and lifted one huge baggy leg and then another, while the man on its back danced and grinned and opened his great eyes wide and shouted. At last I laid a tiny silver coin on a rock, and it put out its trunk and picked up the piece and gave it to the man, who smiled again, and then they went off once more on their slow journey down the middle of the balmy river.

One day we ourselves walked down a rocky river-bed when the water was very low. Overhead were trees heavy with round green fruit which fell and floated, like burnished balls, in the water below. We clambered over smooth wet stones that sometimes had butterflies' wings sticking to them – glistening peacock blue or metallic green. It was all softly silent, only occasionally there came the call of a bird or the sound of fruit dropping into the water. Soon we came to a little cascade, a plume of feathery white falling in the dense dusk of green; and once with a thrill I saw a long black rat-snake lying along the warm surface of a rock. We had almost reached it when it glided into the dark pool below, but when we peered into the clear depth nothing was to be seen.

Above us were swaying creepers, often starred with tiny flowers, hanging from the trees like curtains, like swings, like ropes twisted and strong, and sometimes orchids were growing in them and between the forks of the trees; a little farther on we passed moist patches of ground grown over with ferns and big-leaved spotted caladiums, claret-coloured and veined red, and there it was that I found – ivory in the dark depths of the jungle – pancratium lilies, stiff, erect and fragrant. I picked two or three of the thick-stalked dripping things, and all the way home their faint perfume came up to me on the damp still air.

Another walk that I shall never forget was one along a jungle road at midnight. How wonderful was the silence, the stifling scented stillness of that night! The earth seemed to be drugged by its own scents and heat. I remember, as I went along looking up at the fronds of the palms out-

lined against the crowded starry sky – I remember
how there trailed across the road a scent so sweet,
so strong, that it seemed to concentrate in itself
all the ecstasy of that land, all the intoxication of
the still heavy night.

I stopped and felt my way through the gloom
until I found the flowering tree; I broke off a few
twigs, and when we had light again I saw I held
a kind of rosy stephanotis with long slender
stems and soft velvety leaves. How thickly the
fire-flies glittered in all the trees, carrying their
tiny golden lights high in flying curves. Some
men were fishing in the river with torches and
nets; the fierce orange light fell on their wet bending bodies and lit fitfully the branches soaring
above them. The different lights made a golden
embroidery on the darkness; there were long
golden lines following the ripples on the water;
there were the bright points of gold tracing the
flight of the fire-flies, and in the sky above was
the glitter of the stars.

Only two people stand out in my mind with
any clearness in the long stretch of those solitary
days. One was a wrinkled old man, in discoloured
clothes, who one morning climbed up the verandah steps. He looked poor and battered enough,
but his voice was decided and he carried himself

with dignity. Having bowed, he pulled from out
of his sagging pockets some dirty little bundles,
then undid the dingy wrappings carefully, and
suddenly there sparkled upon the table a small
heap of shining sapphires, all palpitating azure;
next appeared the clear watered green of aqua-
marines; then topazes, flashing rubies, big yellow
tourmalines and brilliant rose-garnets. After these
came handfuls of slippery soft-sheened moon-
stones, milky and clouded, and dull lovely star-
sapphires with their imprisoned floating stars of
light. There they lay in sparkling piles, these
radiant dewdrops of colour, bright jewels blazing
among the bits of old newspaper and rag. And
the shabby old man looked up at us with a faint
smile of invitation.

The other whom I remember is the madman
who lived near the river. He was quite gentle,
they told us; he used to sit under the bridges and
laugh so loudly that you could hear his mirthless
maniacal laughter from a long way off. One day I
was bending down looking at the Sensitive Plant
which grows softly along the side of the road
here, and when I looked up again I saw him
coming along, his dark cloth of striped olive-
green and brown pulled over his head, so that
his wild long hair and wild eyes could hardly be

seen. He was tall and strong, but he walked very slowly. Two or three boys were following him, jumping about and pointing, and throwing pebbles at his feet. Then I saw with peculiar horror that his feet were loosely tied together. I spoke to the boys, and the man stopped for a minute and gazed at us from his other distant world of consciousness. As I met his dazed glance an extraordinary tumult of grief broke over me. In that figure all the helpless misery of the world seemed to be focused, and life seemed drenched with pain. I felt I could never again be as happy as before. 'And no one can help,' I cried out in myself, 'no one since Jesus in Galilee! This man would surely not be like that other madman among the sharp stones of the hill-side, who said: "What have I to do with Thee?" – this man's face is so sad and puzzled. It is asking for help.'

'Anyhow, you are splendid to look at, wasted and helpless as you are. Anyhow, I shall never forget you,' I said to him half aloud, 'never – never!' After a moment he went shuffling on down the road, and the children stopped to look at me instead, thinking me equally mad, no doubt, as I stood there murmuring to myself and blinded by tears.

XIII

IT was on a day of scorching sun broken by
heavy showers that we came to the once royal
city of Kandy. The lake, that slab of green water
lying in the warm lap of green hills, slept in the
heat. At one end of it, steeped in age and quiet,
was the beautiful queer Temple of soft weather-
beaten yellow stone; its yellow reflection in the
water of the moat never rippled. Outside the gate
was a group of jabbering beggars, and inside,
seated on the broad low steps, the halt, the lame
and the blind held out begging-bowls and begging
hands and whined and droned in the hot sunshine. A perpetual plaint rose and fell, but it was
languid as if the heat made even this effort too
great. Half-way up the steps, surrounded by low
trellised walls, was a tank of thick beetle-green
water full of tortoises. The water was choked
with them; they were sacred and torpid; they put
their ageless-looking heads out against the baked
walls and the people dropped food down to them,
leaning idly against the wall, too.

Inside the Temple it was dim and cool, and
fragrant with the scent of spice and flowers. A
few beggars followed us about, their thin Oriental
hands outstretched. We wandered down the

cloisters, where some of the walls were painted
with crude spawling pictures of future punish-
ments for sin. A curious impression of beauty
and slovenliness was given by the mixture of
lovely carven pillars and the litter of faded flowers,
the images of gold and ivory and the floor untidy
and unswept. Creamy heaps of heavy dying
Temple blossoms lay in the dark corners, making
the air oppressive and languorous with their
thick sweetness; the perfume of them hung all
about the courts. In one place under the arcade
young green coco-nuts were piled up in a heap,
and scattered everywhere upon the ground were
long slender flower-tassels from the areca-nut
palm. One could not take a step without treading
upon those tassels of honey-colour or palest
sulphur-green, which I loved to let slide through
my hands and to swing from side to side.

It was a day of festival. The barefooted people
moved about softly, carrying offerings in flat
baskets. Against one wall there stood a row
of Buddhist monks, yellow robes against the
yellowish walls; some followed the people's
movements with their eyes, others waited there
with abstracted looks of gentle reflection. Then
an older monk with a face like a calm Voltaire
came striding down the cloister; wrapped in

a sunflower-coloured robe, he walked disdain-
fully by.

Up at the top of the Temple, in a russet-tiled
tower, there is an octagonal room where the
sacred books are kept. We were taken there by
a priest who went noiselessly before us along the
dark corridor. For a long time we had to stand
at the door, and knock and knock again before it
was slowly opened by a very old monk with a
shaven head and a face like a shrivelled mask, so
little life was there moving behind the eyes. The
room had windows all round looking on to the
lake, and the water threw up a queer yellow-green
light which flooded the room. The sacred books
were much worn, but richly bound in faded
browns and reds and gold. Some, looking very
precious, were wrapped in soft coverings of fine
silk. I wondered if they all told of the starry piety
of the Buddha, but the old monk showed them
very mechanically and without any interest. He
was wishing to be left undisturbed again as soon
as might be. On the table, amongst objects of
gold and alabaster, there was a lovely silvery
bunch of trumpet-flowers and also some clam-
orous-looking paper flowers of light magenta
with unearthly emerald-green leaves. We did
not stay there long; and directly we left we

heard the old priest close and lock the doors behind us.

It was blinding to come down again into the vibrating glare of the full daylight after that dusky dimness. A shower of rain had fallen, leaving all the palm-leaves shining and the heat even damper than before. I stood on the steps looking vaguely at the torpid tortoises and the torpid beggars dozing against the walls, and seeing the natives passing along the road with their clothes, soaked through by the rain, clinging tightly to their bodies. The cream-coloured bullocks, with beads round their meek strong heads, looked like creatures carved in smooth ivory. And then, approaching slowly down the wet red road, came some Kandyan chiefs. It was plain that they were on their way to some function. Their robes were of the thinnest finest muslin embroidered in all bright colours, and had stiffly-padded golden sleeves. Set like platters upon their venerable heads they wore square golden hats that went up into a point. August, enormous, and made ungainly by the yards upon yards of muslin wrapped around them, they came along, each with an attendant behind shading him with a decorated umbrella ; each pegtop figure more unexpected and curious than the last. I stared entranced, feeling that for hours I should like to watch them proceeding in front of the Temple there with the huge umbrellas steadily following too. And yet they had great dignity, a stateliness that not even that ridiculous headgear could destroy. Their deliberate gait, their golden hats, their heavy calm! It was like looking at a rich grotesque frieze which some magic had charmed into a ponderous, slowly-moving life.

Yes, I thought, even in these days there is enough here for the imagination to feast on. To-night, as in the past, the Temple elephants will come out in procession, hung with jewels, hung with garlands, and carry the sacred water to the sacred river through the tropic night. The women dance about them swinging their full skirts of golden-yellow; as they circle they toss up golden balls and catch them again; the torches pour forth flame; the fire rushes upward through the profound soft darkness, and in the leaping light the devil-dancers whirl, furtive and tigerish; their cymbals clash and clang; their panting bodies are streaked with yellow paint; the streaked masks – the streaked skins slung on their backs – all this is real, but oh, how strange, how wild to see!

XIV

I AM waiting for the tropic rain to come down the valley. I am siting at the window looking over the valley. There is thunder over the jungle and over the hills. Here it is very still and very hot. The house has been silent ever since the native 'Boy' came in with his silly face and his silly smile and a silly cap of black and yellow on the back of his head. He wanted to know what the Master would have for breakfast? And Missie? I told him; and after the sound of his bare feet had died away down the passage everything again was still. I am alone in my pink dress near the window; beside me there is a vase of hybiscus and pink lilies. My dress has been faded by the fierce sun. But there is no sun now; it is getting dark; banks of cloud are rolling up and inside them are flickers of lightning. The jungle looks purply-dark; the rain will soon be streaming off all the big leaves; the little paths will be softer than ever and the heavy fragrance more heavy and earthy still. The waves of fragrance wafted over one turn one into another being.

But how many different waves of feeling there are in this tropic island! Waves of terror, waves of lassitude, waves of deep jubilation. Just now I am peaceful, ready to be soaked in the coolness and peace of the rain.

Last month it was different. Last month, when Tim was here, I seemed to be a creature without a soul. Just soulless fruits of the tree of life we seemed to be – or flowers, blossoming, fading, dying. When we walked together in the jungle I seemed to myself, in my pink dress, to be no less light and perishable than any flower. And why shouldn't Tim find this transient thing sweet? And why should I hold back? It was all a fairy-tale – in which nothing mattered. Only I couldn't lose the sense that another greater story was being told – a story of Time and Death and Change; and in that story Jack came too.

But I didn't want to think of Jack, nor to listen to the story which the jungle tells through the hot days and the hot nights, century after century the same. We were so young to be obliged to listen. Tim in his grey flannels and bright tie and sun-hat, did he feel as I did, that this was all a fairy-tale, and that outside the fragile fairy-tale there was doom? One day we were walking along the secret jungle paths, and I had taken off my hat, and had a handful of flowers and ferns picked as we went along. How alone we were in the silence of the daytime. I went on in front under the high flowering trees. The little paths curled in and out, and round rocks with ferns in every cleft, and creepers hung in swaying festoons about us. Tim wanted me to sit down with him; at last he caught my hand. I shook my head. 'I'll stop when I get to the end,' I told him. There was a little door of light and sunshine ahead of us. And there, just at the edge of the jungle, I stopped.

The sun smote down on the colourless withered plain beyond. I sat in the shadow, and he was near behind me.

'Look at me, darling,' he said. 'I want to see again if your eyes are green or blue. No – look at me! I want to see your eyes.'

I hardly heard him. 'How burnt the plains are!' I was thinking. 'The sun soaks into them like rain. And before any men lived here the sun was beating down on this same loneliness.'

I wondered if I should tell Tim what I was thinking about. But what was the use? He was happy, I supposed, thinking about me. He was living deep in the fairy-tale, and I was only half inside it. He moved nearer to me.

'Please don't kiss me,' I said.

Then he began pleading, and I tried to listen, but I couldn't make myself. I seemed to be so swamped in the teeming life of the jungle that I had no life or mind of my own. That heavy mood! How I wished he would wake me out of it! But he couldn't. Perhaps, if we lived here, I thought, this scented earth would lose its power.

What hours we spent together, all in one mood. In the hot daytime we caught quivering lizards that came flashing like bits of emerald enamel from under stones. We ate magenta passion-fruit and picked flowers and chased butterflies. We were even younger than our years; we were children. We watched the chattering natives pick the tea, and in the evening bring in the baskets of fresh young leaves and empty them out. How idly they picked the leaves over. Their coarse dark faces seemed strange and stupid to me. Evening after evening I gazed at them. The pruners' names are taken down, the leaf is weighed, and the names are called: Perimal, Ramen, Veripan, Marimuter.

The head-man has a clever face. And he doesn't chatter like the rest. Their chatter never ceases till they have all gone away, following each other down the little paths winding through the tea.

One night there was a moon. The moonlight glistened down, terribly clear. Tim said: 'Come out. Let's listen to the wanderoos in the jungle. Come! I want to hear the pariah dogs barking at the moon.' And he led me, half in a dream, out into that strange desolation of lonely moonlight.

'From here,' he said, 'you can see even the maidenhair at the bottom of the gully, the moon is so bright – and the wet stones where the cobra lives, and the shrine.'

The sound of the wanderoos came from far, and the sharp querulous barking of the thin dogs in the valley below; and looking down upon the little daubed shrine, I pictured the hideous idol inside – deformed and leering.

The moonlight, which put me into a kind of trance, seemed to flood Tim with excitement.

'I'm going to get on to the rock and shout,' he said. 'I'll scream; and the coolies down there, they'll think it is a devil.'

He climbed the high rock where Vasivuthen beats his dreary tom-tom at the end of the working day, and standing there, his young head lifted, he sent call after call down along the valley – the quiet valley brimmed up with moonlight.

I shivered. 'You frighten me,' I said. 'Please let's go in.' And I told him I felt it dreary out there, with the barking of the monkeys and the hungry dogs, and the fear in the hearts of the people, and the ugly little idol leering in its dark shrine.

'Not yet,' he said, climbing down from the rock. 'Don't go in yet!' he pleaded.

I smiled. I liked to see his grave young face smile whenever I did.

'You must listen to me, darling,' he said. 'You must let me tell you –'

But I wouldn't. 'Please let's go in,' I said. Only he wouldn't let me. He stood laughing in front of the little door with both arms out.

Well, he has gone now. I wonder if I ought to have been different while he was here. I couldn't respond to his feeling any more than I could repel it. To me it was all one with the heavy fragrance and the listless warmth. All the time he was with us I moved as in an opium dream. Like a child I was led by him here and there. But at last we made him go away. For he had come from England to see the world, and so far he had clung to this tiny lonely spot. We made him go. I went a little way down the road with him. We went along past the hedge of orange tangapou and past the tree ferns, he leading his horse slowly along. It was evening; there was no sun to strike on our bare heads. The coolies were walking along the road in twos and threes. I stopped to say good-bye. And the coolies gathered nearer as we stood still. He looked so tall amongst them – proud-faced and slender. He gazed at me, and the dark faces around gazed wonderingly at us. We seemed to be suspended in a motionless bubble of Time – so still it was.

Then he dropped the reins from his hand and turned full to me with the same question in his eyes. No movement, no sound came from those dark figures standing by. I shook my head. He mounted and rode away: the bubble of Time broke and life moved on again.

XV

THE rain has come now; every leaf drips heavily. I wonder if it cools the trodden, ruined space in that other jungle far away, where we went to see the ending of the great drive of elephants. That time, when I look back on it, seems rather hateful to me – the torrid days and thirsting nights, the dusty trapped animals, and the stinging insects.

After leaving the train we had a long drive in a bullock-cart which bumped along the rough track through the jungle. The driver flicked at the black bullocks and shouted at them incessantly. They went at a very slow trot, but it shook the springless cart mercilessly, jolting us and our boxes this way and that. We bought some green coco-nuts, I remember, and drank every drop of the milk eagerly.

A sort of village had been built in the jungle and crowds of natives had collected to see the last act. Everything had been made out of palm-leaves: there was even a palm-leaf post office and a palm-leaf hotel. Little huts had been put up for us, in which we each had a tiny room with just a camp-bed and a chair. Outside, perched on three sticks, was a basin to wash in. Such

light as there was came in through the flimsy
leaf door.

In the evening we went to look at the stockade,
which was concealed amongst the trees and thorny
bushes. It had a very wide neck that gradually
narrowed down and made an entrance to a round
space enclosed by a wall of great posts and crossed
logs tied together with jungle rope. Towards this
mouth the herd of wild elephants had been driven
night by night for weeks by an army of beaters.
And now at last they were said to be quite near
the hidden opening.

On our way to the place we met tame elephants
lumbering along the narrow paths with branches
of trees or enormous sheaves of green stuff tucked
under their trunks. Others, tied up for the night,
were eating the gathered fodder and treading
everything down flat round them. Fat brown
babies, belonging to their keepers, played amongst
them, talking shrilly and running in and out
between the massive legs.

Later on, when night came, I found it difficult
to go to sleep, and lying on my camp-bed through
the hot night I listened to the trumpeting of the
wild elephants, which at times drowned the con-
tinuous whirring of the insects. Rifles, too, were
occasionally fired off, and sometimes the yells and

howls of the beaters rose to such a frantic pitch that one imagined the whole herd must be charging back.

In the morning we went to the stockade again, and then it was said that the elephants would all be in by the afternoon. Certainly the shouting and shooting did now sound very close indeed. So we waited, crouching down as we were told. Occasionally a beater would run forward, gesticulating wildly, signal to every one to keep quiet and rush back again. One of the head-men of the district was beating too; I had seen him before and heard him speaking a careful pedantic English. It was odd to see him now, nearly naked, his long hair twisted up behind his head, a great rifle in his hand, rushing in and out of the jungle. His body was glistening with sweat and he was shouting instructions, but occasionally he stopped politely to talk with some one in his precise English.

At last the whisper went round that the herd was actually in the mouth of the stockade. But alas! the next report was that an old elephant who first had gone in, recognizing it for a trap, had come out again, and that this had turned the whole herd back. It seemed little use trying to move them forward again just then.

By this time we were getting rather tired.

There was very little shade under those thin trees; the sun beat down upon the parched crackling ground and struck up again into one's face; a matted prickly undergrowth spread everywhere. The beaters, too, were beginning to lose heart. They sent word to one of their priests to call upon the Elephant God. A thin man close to us stepped out from the crowd. After declaiming loudly for a few minutes he pressed his high cap firmly on to his head and broke into a clumsy dance. Round and round he went while his friends chanted and beat tom-toms in a circle about him. In the end he fell into a kind of trance and declared that the elephants would not come in of themselves that day. But, he added, he wasn't afraid of wild elephants; they would recognize him as an elephant-priest. So he would go and put a spell on them and force them to come in.

An avenue was made through the awed and admiring crowd and the poor man disappeared proudly into the trees – his last triumphant moment of life! For he went on, we were afterwards told, right up to the place where the elephants had gathered. There, with his arms raised high, he solemnly conjured them to follow him. Pathetic faith in his calling! One of the elephants lifted him up with its trunk and dashed him to the ground. He was dead, and afterwards they carried him back and laid him in the thorny jungle.

That night the little booths of the impromptu village were lit by large flares, and before them the brightly clad crowd passed and re-passed. The wares were chiefly brilliant rolls and bundles of stuff, fruits and vegetables, and bottles of raw-coloured drinks. The rows of saffron, ruby-red and wry pink drinks glowed in that harsh light. One or two white planters were strolling about singing; bullock-carts jolted along with their grunting, grumbling drivers; some men sat by the wayside reading to themselves in high sing-song voices; the noosers, huge men with hairy legs, swaggered up and down in the middle of the road. These were experts who had come from a long way off to noose the elephants when they were at last trapped.

It was curious undressing in one's little hot den with its floor of the same pebbly sand as the road outside, along which one heard the people walking and talking. The next morning when my 'Boy' brought me the very small ration of brownish water that was allowed for the day, he told me that the herd was safely in the stockade. They had been driven in during the night when all was quiet. So as soon as we had had breakfast we

hurried off there, and clambered up into a little
platform that had been built in the trees. At last
we saw them! There they were – a moving mass
of elephants, huddling and circling about in the
middle of the enclosure trying to get as far as
possible from the noisy crowd of people that surrounded them. The trees that were left standing in
the space they had already trampled so bare were
dusty green, the elephants dusty grey. They
looked inexpressibly weary. Among them were a
good many big ones. One young bull had been
killed just outside the gate of the stockade because
he kept charging back.

Fires had been lighted all round the edge of the
enclosed ground, and there the beaters now sat
resting, their rifles and long sticks by them, ready
to shout and yell should an animal come anywhere
near the side. For the wall of the stockade was
mere bluff, as we soon saw, for one of the tame
elephants inside the enclosure happened to take
fright at a rifle shot and came plunging towards
us. With trunk up and ears lifted, it paused a
moment in front of the wall of great logs and
branches, then lunged forward and went through
as if it were matchwood. The people fled in all
directions. And on it went! I never knew that
elephants could career like that. Straight into the

jungle it disappeared, the mahout on its back clinging there like a scared monkey.

It was exciting to watch the noosing, which was done by two gangs which went out in turn. A couple of trained elephants would advance, separate one of the animals from the rest of the herd, and then manœuvre to get one on each side of it. The wild elephant would either keep moving slowly on in front or dodge, or, if it were fierce, wheel round and charge. A man with a noose of very thick rope in his hand came crouching behind one or other of the tame elephants; it was his part to run out, when the wild one's back was turned, and slip the noose round its leg as it lifted its foot. Sometimes this was quickly done, sometimes it took a long time. Occasionally the noose would slip off, and once or twice an unusually strong elephant managed to break the rope. When, however, the nooser had been successful and both the animal's hind legs had been noosed, the two decoys twisted the rope round the trunk of a thick tree and began to pull at it slowly and steadily. The crowd yelled to see the wild creature, which never before had gone any way but its own, now being dragged slowly backwards – much to its surprise and fear. Some elephants would begin trumpeting loudly, most horrible to hear; others

[136]

fell down upon their knees. But it always ended in the same way: they were tied up to the tree and there left to struggle and pull, to heave and strain, until one thought those grey, loose, huge legs must surely come out of their sockets or the tree crack and fall. It was a horrid sight. It shamed one to see them, pulling and pulling at the rope and falling heavily forward on their trunks, and then stopping exhausted, and throwing the hot sand over their great heaving streaming sides.

It took a long time to secure the big bull of the herd. The rope broke twice, and he kept charging the decoys and making short dashes for the stockade wall, only to be turned back by the shouting and firing.

We spent most of the day upon our platform, and in the evening, after a pale full moon had floated up, we went back to the stockade. No breath of wind stirred; there fell no moisture of dew; and the thought of the trapped elephants made us wretched, although we knew they would be well treated later on.

The scene by night was unforgettable; the red ring of fires lighted on the ground; the men crouching round them; the glow on dark faces, long hair, bare bodies; the blankets laid on the earth and the rifles lying near by. Red clay pots full of rice were being cooked for the evening meal; the flames lit up twisted trunks of trees and dry creepers hanging down.

By the misty white light of the moon you could just see the tops of the trees swaying in the middle of the stockade and make out dark massive forms tramping slowly, silently, round and round. Like creatures in a dream, all those that had not been noosed kept silently moving in that much-trampled space. Bewildered and exhausted, they kept close to one another. For a long time I looked at them and then again at the burning circle of fires, and I thought how little the crowd could do to disturb the vast stillness of the jungle stretching mile upon mile under the white moon-light.

We had started out on this expedition gaily enough, but a feeling of sadness had now crept in. Poor elephants! you are caught at last; the driving, relentless for six weeks, has stopped; you are allowed the peace of a prison, the quietness of a cage.

The next morning we were guided through the thorny undergrowth to the place where the elephant had been shot. There it lay, a great grey block, with just one bullet-wound between its eye and ear. I can see it now so clearly lying on the hot ground there just as it had fallen: the large ears flat back, the little eye dimmed, the thick dusty skin all wrinkled. A man in nothing but a loin-cloth and a dull indigo turban sat cross-legged on the ground beside it, patiently sawing off the feet. His bare body glistened beside that lifeless grey mass; his eyes shone; he spat red betel-juice through his reddened teeth. Still sawing away, he looked up at us with a smile. The feet, he said, would make charms that brought luck. And I was faintly comforted to think that the poor elephant was to be of some little use after all; it seemed such a big thing to kill and leave. Perhaps this rain is falling there now and washing those broad bones white.

The elephants having all been safely tethered, the whole of kraal town dispersed in one day. The bullock-carts, stuffed with bedding and boxes, jolted away to the railway siding. All along the narrow track there was an unbroken stream of people eager to get back out of the jungle to their homes. But at the station many were left behind, including our luckless Boy, who rushed at door after door along the train, only to be repulsed at each and hurled backwards on to the platform.

All through the burning afternoon the little

train panted through dry jungle; occasionally
there came a puff of aromatic scent; occasionally
one saw above the scrubby bushes a tree with
flaring coral flowers; otherwise everything was
brown, sparse-coloured, withered. Covered with
dust, we talked spasmodically of elephants, heat,
insects, drinks. Whenever we stopped, all the
passengers at once swarmed on to the platform
like locusts and bought every green coco-nut or
bottle of soda-water that was to be seen. All along
in the cruel glare one saw thirsty planters in sun-
hats, and pale women greedily drinking coco-nut-
milk or sharing tepid bottles of lemonade.

In the evening the train drew up at a small
station, where we got out to wait for the night
mail. It came presently, thundering along out of
the soft velvety darkness. Very tired, but sleepless,
I sat by the open window and looked out into the
night. I thought of the thorny jungle we had just
left, and of the dead elephant and the dead elephant-priest lying in it; I thought of the other
glorious creatures I had lately seen overcome by
men: the heavy bear in the fragrance of the Himalayan forest happily shaking the apricot trees;
the young tiger with its shuddering roar, beating
desperately against iron bars; and now these
elephants pulling and pulling and falling in the

dust. Human beings, with all their litter, chatter and brutality, seemed hardly worthy of their greater power. How unattractive we had appeared, heated, jabbering, and fighting for places in the train!

But, as the train climbed higher and the heat lessened, all the ugliness of the last few days fell away from me. Dawn came, and with it beauty again at last. With delight I saw once more the soft green grass in the shady coco-nut-groves – green grass and the lines of graceful stems crowned by feathery fronds, with orange and green nuts clustering in the centre and thick rinds lying on the ground below; I saw, too, the waxy-white splendour of trumpet-flowers in lonely thickets opening to the sun; I saw the pure blue 'morning glory' against the azure hills. How refreshing, how cool was the air! and before the sun had risen much farther I went to sleep.

XVI

I THOUGHT I should be all alone at the hotel before getting on to the boat. Richard had gone back to India the day before by another route, so I arrived at the seaport by myself. All day, sitting by the window of the slow train, I had gazed out at the gradually changing landscape. At first I looked down on white waterfalls and wet rocks fringed with ferns, on grey curtains of rain that parted to disclose wide warm spaces of earth and sun and cloud. Then, as we dropped lower, I saw the flat paddy-fields with white paddy-birds flapping above them; I saw the pale tassels of areca-nut palms hanging down in the motionless air, and beyond them the blue of the distance, the soft, rich blue of the windless noonday. The stations were flowery with sweet, coloured garlands of creepers; oily-skinned natives came along the platforms with trays of green coco-nuts and coloured drinks and their call of water.

We ran down into the station an hour before sunset. I got out feeling confused after the long silence, and was glad to escape from the crowd of chattering natives who surged along the platform. Outside there was magic in the soft evening air. After the hills the damp brooding heat made all smells and sounds seem different and more intense.

It was the first time I had stayed at a hotel alone, and I can remember my arrival with great distinctness: the hall with its long chairs where men were drinking iced drinks; the big windows through which the harbour water gleamed; the impassive Malay clerk with his parchment face; the long dim passage with white figures of servants squatting outside doors and the cool bareness of my own room.

A ship had just come in. When I went down into the hall again a group of travellers were standing by the office counter, and as I was walking past I recognized one of them. It was George Seaton, an acquaintance of Richard's, who was married and whom I had met once or twice in England and then once or twice again out here. What fun to find a friend, I said to myself; and just at that moment he looked up and caught sight of me.

'So you *are* here!' he cried. 'That's luck. I wondered if I'd catch you. Where are the others – and Richard?'

I explained how I came to be there by myself.

'Well, I'll look after you,' he replied. 'But your

boat is a day late. It won't be in till midnight to-morrow at the earliest.'

I was a little dashed by this news; for one thing, I didn't like him well enough to want to be alone with him for long.

'Let's dine together!' he went on. And I answered: 'Do let's,' for there was really nothing else to say.

He had suddenly made me feel childish as I stood by him there. In contrast with Tim he was oppressive and dominating. 'These are my last hours out here,' I thought sadly, 'and they will all be coloured by him.'

I dressed and found him waiting in the hall. He came up and complimented me on my dress. It was an old dress, I told him, which I had put on because it reminded me of home. I was feeling shy, and in the dining-room, as I looked across the table at George, his bantering looks and lazy talk made me shyer and shyer. I stared out of the big open window and felt a longing to escape. Outside, over the warm ocean, burning clouds were flung in all directions across the sky; they looked like rose-pink feathers tossed up against the luminous blue.

'Has your time in India changed you?' asked George. 'Are you nicer or not so nice?'

'Just weaker,' I answered. And at that moment I was indeed feeling very weak. I was thinking, too, that somehow his time in the East had not improved him.

After dinner he led the way outside; a listless breeze, soft from the sea, blew languidly about us and stirred the divine warmth of the night. I saw a carriage with an old white horse waiting.

'I'm going to take you for a drive,' he said. 'It's the only thing to do when it's as hot as this.'

I looked before me, silent.

'Come!' he said.

But suddenly a wave of resolution swept over me and I shook my head. Before he had time to protest, I said good night and ran upstairs to my room.

Once there, I sat down by the window, too tired to do anything but look vaguely out over the quiet harbour and the broad red road with the waiting carriages and sleeping drivers hunched up by them. I felt lonely almost to the point of tears.

Nor could I sleep that night; it was too hot for sleep. The stars glittered between the fronds of the palms, jet-black against the jewelled sky. These same far burning suns, I thought, are shining now into those deep gorges where the Oxus flows strongly, and on the great wall stretching over China, and on the windy monasteries of Tibet with the little ragged flags flying in the starlight, on the steaming swamps of New Guinea and on the thick forests where the Brahmaputra is rushing – on so much of this little earth of ours which to those suns is nothing. And all my old terror of the stars and space came flooding back to me.

The next day the heat was yet heavier. Outside in the scorching street the languid shopkeepers stood motionless before the doors of their shaded shops of precious stones, of sandalwood and tortoise-shell, sometimes mechanically offering sapphires or cat's-eyes to people passing by. Opposite the hotel sat a snake-charmer with his covered basket beside him. His face, under his orange turban, was wet; the hooded cobra erect in front of him looked dusty and small.

When George came up to me and said he would take me to the Botanical Gardens in the evening, I agreed to go. We started after tea. Whiffs of garlic, whiffs of spice, came from the shops as we drove past. And at every scent and sound and sight I thought: 'This is the last time. To-morrow I shall be far away.' How familiar were the flat baskets of grain and fruit, the rough heavy jack-fruit and brinjals, smooth and smoky-purple. Familiar, too, were the piled bales of cloth with their borders of gold and vermilion. But one sight I saw was new to me: a medicine-man came down the street; his face was painted with streaks of colour and he walked clumsily on stilts. A green basket-like hat was on his head and he droned out a sort of chant. His follower carried a bowl, and the people ran out from their houses to put grain and money into it.

Presently we came out of the town on to a dusky flowery road and passed under a temple-tree in full bloom. Some of the milk-white blossoms had fallen on to the grass. I asked the driver to stop and got out to pick them up, for they seemed to give me the very essence of this fragrant land. But as I was filling my hands with them, feeling that not one waxy petal could be left behind, a thick flat snake crawled sluggishly across the road just in front of me. Dropping all the flowers, I fled back to the carriage. George laughed when he found that I was trembling. I tried to explain that it was not the snake by itself that had frightened me, but that the snake had seemed to bring to the surface all sorts of vaguer underground fears.

'But what exactly are you frightened of?' he persisted.

'Everything,' I said helplessly. And I meant that everything in life seemed too pressing, too vivid – living and dying, loving and – worse still – not loving – everything was overwhelming – especially beneath the stupendous stars which are never hidden here.

By the gate of the Gardens there was a twisted tree of scarlet blossoms. A shaven Buddhist priest was passing along, his boy disciple walking behind him. The boy stooped, picked up one of the fallen flowers and gave it to me, and the priest looked on with the smallest possible smile on his calm, gentle face.

There seemed to be no one inside the Gardens excepting ourselves. We went slowly up an avenue of trees, whose huge rosy flowers hung down like bells above our heads. George had been silent for a long time, and now I noticed that he was oppressed and sombre.

At the end of the avenue we came suddenly upon a big pool. Fluttering round it were moon-moths and on the edge of it grew moon-flowers. Palest moths and palest flowers! Like everything else, they were soaked in the green-gold air of the evening. Their lovely fragility seemed to become

[148]

almost solid in the light that lay heavily upon the still pool. The lotus leaves looked as though they were forged out of some heavy metal – tarnished bronze, they lay upon a surface of tarnished gold. The lotus flowers were of pearl held aloft on stalks of jade. Only the white birds that flew over the water were airy and light.

As I stood there I forgot George completely, and then when I glanced at him again he was staring moodily at the ground. I realized that he was very sad, and noticed how much older he looked than when I had known him in England.

'This time to-morrow you will be on your way home,' he said.

I felt sorry for him because of the envy in his voice; but I also half-envied him. I looked up into the nutmeg trees under which we were now passing; never again should I see the yellowish nutmegs amongst the glossy green nor smell the faint smell of the dry leaves and rinds below. How much there was here that I should remember with longing as keen almost as home-sickness.

'Yes,' he went on heavily, 'you are going home. But I – I shall be old when the time comes for me to go. And it won't mean to me then what it would mean now.'

The rough gloom of his tone frightened me, but I answered as lightly as I could.

We walked on in silence and all around us there was a deep hush. Great ochre thunder-clouds had been piling themselves up in the south and now heavy single drops began to fall. In the distance we heard thunder; lightning, too, made a flicker in the air.

George pointed to a garden-house near by. The bougainvilia festooning the verandah looked theatrically magenta in the lurid light. Hardly had we time to take shelter before the storm crashed and broke above us. Flashes of harsh blue light lit up the swaying coco-nut trees; the palm fronds soughed and drooped under the beating shafts of rain. Our verandah was soon flooded; I stood in water with my white dress clinging wetly about me. George, leaning against the rough yellow-washed wall, appeared to be fighting some battle in his mind. I turned away from him; I watched a bedraggled jackal slink across a glade between the oleanders, looking over its shoulder in the frightened way they do.

The rain stopped with suddenness and at once the earth began to steam. The steaming air was made more languorous still by the smell of a gardenia just under the verandah. I looked down into its cool flowers that were full of shining drops.

Without turning round, I said: 'We had better go back.'

He did not seem to hear; he muttered something about the loneliness of his life. I looked out over the darkening garden. The misery in his mind linked itself with the heat and the damp and woke in me a kind of answering nightmare. I knew something would happen; it did not surprise me when he caught up my hands and hid his face in them.

I stood still in a daze. I could do nothing, nor find any word to give him comfort. Our minds were too far apart. I pitied him; but all the time I was thinking vaguely of Jack. I thought how he, too, was exiled in these lands of fever and strain; how he, too, had wanted something of me, but not even to him had I given a crumb of comfort.

In utter misery and confusion I murmured: 'I'm wretched, too! I'm wretched, too!' And as I spoke I felt that I could not bear to live my life alone. When I was alone the pain of the whole world seemed to beat in on me. I could not be alone.

The next moment, before I could move, he had

seized and kissed me. And at once everything became even more like a sick dream. I seemed to have been standing there for ever; and for ever the steamy garden would continue to steam before my eyes.

As soon as George let me go I seemed to forget him. As we went draggingly back to the waiting carriage my mind was full of the thought of home. Absently I stared at the red road splashing red mud; at the blossoms dashed off the trees and lying torn in the way; at the soaked houses which seemed to glow with a curious intensity. 'This is the end!' I kept saying to myself. 'This is the end! To-morrow I shall be far out, steaming across the blue, blue emptiness of ocean. All this fever will die down in those long vacant days. The days will come and pass by unbrokenly; there will be nothing to trouble me. I shall be as I was upon the voyage out. I shall forget this day -- and all the things I want to forget – as one forgets one's dreams.'

XVII

A June morning in England, and I am home
again. This glittering summer rain will soon be
over, and meanwhile it is peaceful to sit by the
window and look out once more at all the familiar
things. The chestnuts are raising their white
pyramids of flowers against leaves that are the
heavy blue-green of tapestry; drifts of light cow-
parsley are heaped up under the tall elms, and the
elms are green with little leaves still light and
fresh. Down by the river the ardent marsh-mari-
golds are growing loosely in the boggy places,
filling with yellow the trickling wet ditches.
What happiness I had yesterday walking across
those whispering water-meadows of juicy grass
and flowers! How joyfully I saw again the curly
alder trees, the willows whitening and the poplars
turning silvery at every little air that rose and
died away! How I rejoice in the sweet, fresh
intimacy of England!

In the afternoon there was a little horse show
going on in the park: flags flying round a ring, and
in the sunshine the farmers' sons riding their
spirited horses – young men with strong arms
and ruddy faces, their white shirts fluttering in
the breeze. The heavy country crowd stood

pressed against the railings, cheering, laughing, and flinching backwards whenever the horses galloped by. Now they stared at the great ample cart-horses that were led solemnly round, the owners patting the strong curved necks, the silky coats smooth over rippling muscles. The band played loudly, the little pennons blew gaily in front of the wall of trees, and above the wood rose a bank of clouds, dazzlingly white and solid against the blue of the sky. I couldn't help smiling all the time I was there: everything was so pastoral and so soothing, everything was happening in the traditional fashion, even the pale moon floating above looked as if she belonged to the place and would never wander off to lands far away.

But at the end of the day the band began to play a tune which that other band had played at those other sports at the baked cantonments in India. I saw Jack lying back in the chair by my side, outwardly so languid, but with that dreadful tenseness I always felt in him. Again the restlessness of his mind was communicated to me, and again I felt the strain of the sun's palpitating glare. It made everything around me here seem too soft and well-arranged.

The show was over. Evening brought out

from the June meadows a delicious scent which breathed through the smell of horses and trodden grass and coarse tobacco. The people moved slowly away, stopping in groups to watch the animals being led back to the village. Full of troubled thoughts, I went up the road along which I had driven on that late autumn day before starting for India. And I remembered how, when putting on my bridal dress for the play, I seemed to see the people and the places of the future circling round me, and then found myself alone in the end. Yes! that loneliness had come true: not even Jack's intensity had been able to draw me out of my own inner world with its visions of beauty which were my joy and its loneliness which was my pain.

Turning aside, I went up into the great garden near by. The evening deepened; in the empty garden the last rays of the sun fell on a bed of azaleas, shining through their fragile blossoms of lemon-yellow, apricot and pink. 'The vague fragrance of them is like this country,' I thought. 'It can awaken no wild longing. How different from the fierce or languorous perfumes of the East. Is it already over, the happiness of returning? There are moments – and this is one – when England seems pale and mild and grey. There are no ardours here, I feel, no tigers, no madmen, no scorching suns, no stupendous snows, no ash-covered figures staring at one from a fanatical world of their own. Here everything is well understood, well tended, well loved. Even the earth is closely clothed with grass to the very foot of the trees, to the very brink of the cliffs. Here is just the easy English kindness with all the sharpness of life and feeling blunted and softened.'

I walked on, and the transience of everything on this earth – of men and beasts and flowers – stabbed my mind with a violent, sudden grief. I thought of the persons and places past which I had drifted unchanged – those chance encounters, those loose ends of friendship, those rivers pouring away and away, those places which had seemed charged with an inward significance – a significance that one possessed but for a single instant. And the flame of life did seem to me then, as to the Rajah's A.D.C., 'nothing but a candle in the wind'.

Turning, I went along a disused shrubbery-walk where the stored-up dampness of wet days breathed a chill into the air. The light filtered so scantily through the foliage that I thought the sun must have set behind clouds, but suddenly at a turn in the path the shrubs fell away and there before me lay a rich space of country drenched in exultant light. On the grassy slopes the bronzed deer were feeding amongst the bronzed patches of bracken, the massed trees stood dreaming in utter quietness through the endless June evening, and the hills beyond were turning from deep to deeper blue.

And then again, as once before in that hot moonlit station in India, there opened out a sudden way of deliverance. The disquiet of the past months fell away from me. I knew there was permanence: I felt reality. A bubble of eternity had risen through time and held me for an instant in its shining peace. 'I shall find them again,' I said to myself, 'the flowers and jungles and innocent huge beasts. I shall find them where the pattern of these things eternally dwells.'

ABOUT CONSTANCE SITWELL

by
John A Ferguson

Constance Mary Evelyn Talbot was born in August 1887 in Ceylon. Although her year of birth is generally given as 1888, in her book *Bounteous Days* she refers to her 'birthday of 1908 when I was twenty-one.'

She was always known to her friends as "Conty". She lived in Ceylon from her birth in 1888 until 1897 and always retained a love of its beauty, colours, flowers and scents. From the age of 13 she kept diaries which reveal her independent and inquiring mind.

After the family returned to England from Ceylon they lived at Harpenden, Herts., for seven years. Then from 1904 they lived at Marchmont, near Hemel Hempstead, Herts. In January 1910 Constance and her parents returned to Ceylon for a holiday.

Between 1906 and 1911 Constance stayed a number of times at Renishaw, Derbyshire and at Scarborough with Sir George and Lady Ida Sitwell and their children Edith (b.

1887), Osbert (b. 1892) and Sacheverell (b. 1897). The three children were the third cousins once removed of her (yet to be met) future husband.

Before her marriage Constance Talbot was pursued by a number of 'my young men' who saw themselves as potential suitors. These included Arnold Sandwith Ward M.P. (1876-1951) the son of (Thomas) Humphry Ward (1845-1926) and the novelist Mary Augusta Ward, née Arnold (1851-1920), who wrote under the name of Mrs. Humphry Ward. They lived at 'Stocks', near Aldbury, Hertfordshire, where Constance stayed on a number of occasions. Many of her male friends were killed in the early years of the First World War.

In January 1912, Constance Talbot went to India, with her mother, to see her brother Humphrey who was stationed at Lahore. Hunting was a popular past-time with the military and, although she had never hunted before, Constance accompanied the wife of the Colonel of the 17th Lancers on a hunt on 16 February 1912. Hunting was the equivalent to British fox-hunting although in Lahore the prey was the jackal.

Whilst on a hunt she met Colonel William Henry Sitwell D.S.O. of Barmoor Castle, Northumberland who was on the staff of the 3rd Lahore Division. During that hunt the jackal had given a run of seven miles in 25 minutes and at the end William presented the jackal's mask (head) and the bush (tail) to the two ladies.

Colonel Sitwell was a widower who had been posted to India in 1909; his first wife had been Constance Selina Meade (1875-1908). He was the son of Major Francis Henry Massey Sitwell (1831-69) of Barmoor Castle and Elizabeth Maria D'Olier (1832-1917). He later became Brigadier-General William Henry Sitwell of Barmoor Castle C.B., D.S.O., D.L., J.P.

Constance wrote of this fateful hunt: 'How new it all is! Soldiering mixed with hunting is practically the whole life of those I am with now. Nearly everyone rides – everyone English that is to say, and every one seems to be the same sort of age. There are no old people here, and scarcely any children... I hadn't been here two days before I was made to hunt. My brother, whom I had now joined, had got a pony for me; and still feeling slightly bewildered I started off with him before dawn for the first day's meet. It was in the cool starlight that we set out. We crowded into a carriage...After a while we reached a bridge over a canal and saw a ring of horses standing, and a ring of muffled syces hunched round a fire that they had lighted on the ground to keep warm by. We got out stiffly and mounted; then voices were heard and we saw the shadowy hounds coming along the canal bank and behind them more people riding. But how quickly after dawn the day grew hot and glaring! We jumped endless ditches and banks, and at last they killed the jackal they were hunting, with its cowed and pointed face. It looked so thin compared with the hounds.'

Constance and her mother had been staying in an hotel and William Sitwell invited them to stay with him for three nights. Mrs. Talbot and Constance arrived on 20th February. They used William's residence as a base and stayed for three weeks - until the 13th of March. William learnt that they had visited the Sitwells at Renishaw just after he and his mother had been there during the summer of the previous year. [The Talbots had stayed at Renishaw in August 1911.] While they were staying with him, William took the two ladies to a number of functions and spent some time with Constance. For example he had 'two delightful rides before breakfast' on 3rd and 4th March, 'with Miss Talbot...plenty to look at for the observing eye which I'm bound to say the girl has.' He remarked that it was not unpleasant to have ladies in the house and that 'the Talbot girl' was 'certainly very well informed and nice.' Mrs. Talbot and Constance prepared to return to England in mid-March. William wrote to his mother on 12th March 1912; 'I shall miss them greatly. She is such a beautiful old lady and the daughter...is charming, quite pretty and very clever. Moreover her name is Constance so I rather love her.' On 14th March he wrote, 'Yesterday the Talbot's left me and the house feels empty. I took the girl for a ride through the bazaar before breakfast and drove them later through the city in the afternoon which interested them enormously. They had previously seen only one thoroughfare of it from the back of an elephant. The only way to see things is from a carriage at a fast pace. Dined with them at their hotel.' The Talbots left Lahore on Saturday 16th March 1912 ready to return to England.

In April 1912 William was himself back in England and made his base the Naval & Military Club, 94, Piccadilly, London. By the 10th May, Mrs. Talbot and Constance had come up to London. William took Constance out on a number of occasions, for example to see a ventriloquist – she had never been to a music hall before – and the ballerina Anna Pavlova. Her parents regarded William as a 'properly reliable chaperone.' By the end of May they were engaged. The engagement ring was, 'one of Mrs Newman's best efforts. She fell in love with Conty on the spot naturally enough.'

William returned to his military duties in India, sailing on 31st May and arrived at the Bombay Taj Mahal Palace Hotel on 14th June 1912. From thence he went to his posting at St. Ann's, Ootacamund, which was located in the Nilgiri Hills. His address was: 'Head Quarters Southern Army, Ootacamund, India.'

William wrote to his mother on 17th August, 'Conty God bless her ought to reach Aden tomorrow morning after breakfast. Trust and hope that the worst of the Monsoon is now over and she won't have a bad time twixt Aden and Bombay…Conty reports in her last letter from Marchmont that she had been staying at Ashridge where there was a large gathering of her aristocratic relations. All of whom gave her presents and heard her letters. Lord Brownlow, who must be a delightful man, returned thanks on my behalf.'

William was in Bombay on 19th August where he met and dined with Constance's brother Humphrey. The following day William met Constance on board the ship on which she had arrived from England and by 9am her 'very moderate' baggage was unloaded. They made their way to Bombay Cathedral where the Padre 'made the necessary affidavits' and they 'were quietly, decently and solemnly married by 10.45.'

They were married on 20th Aug 1912 in St. Thomas' Cathedral, Bombay, India.

The Times had an incorrect date in its marriage notice:

SITWELL: TALBOT – On the 23 Aug., at the Cathedral Bombay COLONEL WILLIAM SITWELL, C.B., D.S.O., of Barmoor Castle, Northumberland to CONSTANCE EVELYN MARY, younger daughter of Mr. and Mrs. Gustavus Talbot of Marchmont House, Hemel Hempstead, Herts.

At the time of their marriage Constance was 25 years old and William was aged 51.

After their marriage they stayed at the Taj Mahal Palace Hotel, Bombay where they had dinner and the following day had 'lunch in at the Joint Club where a band was playing and we are very happy.'

They arrived at St. Ann's, Ootacamund on 27th August where William wrote, 'Here we are at last...Conty positively enchanted with it all and says it is fairy land which I told her it would be... I walked her round them *(the grounds)* and as always she returned with her hands full of all sorts of odd wild flowers...Conty is as excited as a child with all the new things there are to see...she avers (it) is exactly like Ceylon...She really is an inexhaustible joy to me and one of the most observant people I have ever met as I found out long ago and reported to you I think... Humphrey Talbot will have reached Ooty *(Ootacamund)* today I hope and tomorrow leaves St Ann's for appointment at the Club by Conty's command as she doesn't want him in the house for a few days till she has settled down.'

On 5th December 1912 Constance wrote a letter to William's mother Elizabeth Sitwell:

Dear Mrs Sitwell,

You will get a letter from Willie this week from the manoeuvres. He has been gone almost a fortnight now – and I miss him so much – but there is only one more week alone.

I have been staying at Government House & with some other people; and tomorrow am going to stay with the General's wife, who is also left alone – People are extraordinarily kind here when they think one is lonely. It makes a great difference not having a garden to walk about in – there is nowhere but the road - & that is so dusty –

I used to paint a good deal in the garden at Gov: House – there was a lovely grove of orange and lemon trees there, & avenues of apple trees. Christmas week here seems to be a famous time; the place is crowded with people - & such as can't get rooms live in tents. There is a regular programme made using morning, afternoon & evening – but I don't think Willie & I will attend to it all.

FLOWERS AND ELEPHANTS

The bear skin, which was sent away to be made into a rug has come back – and is very fine indeed. It was luck just shooting it, as we only stopped at the place for one night. I thought that week in the Himalayas was most wonderful; the forests seemed so endless & fragrant & silent - & the hill-people so delightful with soft voices. I saw one or two Rajahs when I was at Government House, but none so nice as Willie's friend at Chamba. They do have such beautiful jewellery and rings.

I think Willie is enjoying being out-of-doors all day; he writes to me on little bits of paper while he is sitting under a tree – or from 'the field of battle' as he says.

I hope you are quite well - & that Miss Clem is better too – I did write to her once – but I haven't had a letter from her yet.

Willie does not seem at all sure as to what is going to happen to him after March. It would be nice to know a little bit but I do look forward to being in England in April and for the Summer – I am beginning to feel as if I know my way about Barmoor a little bit because he so often talks of it & the country around; I think the lawn must be loved & the wild cherry trees.

Willie always reads your letters to me – I am so glad you like the photograph. I hope you will have a happy Christmas.

With much love – from Conty

In April 1913, William and Constance Sitwell were in England where their first child Constance Anne was born. In October they returned to India and daughter Anne remained in England with her grandmother for some months before she was brought to India. William was in command of the Quetta 1st Infantry Brigade in Baluchistan between 1913 and 1914. He became Temporary Brigadier General in November 1913. In a letter to her mother-in-law, Mrs Elizabeth Sitwell, in December 1913 Constance refers to Quetta as being the Northumberland of India. However, in her diaries (*Bounteous Days*, published 1976) she paints a different picture and refers to the area as being 'very alien to me, rocky and arid, with plane trees planted in rows and dry, hot air. There was no grass, or anything damp.' Their accommodation was 'a large house and treeless garden with a shrivelled lawn...' Shortly after the World War of 1914 began they were ordered back to England.

Their children were:

1. Constance Anne Sitwell (1913-81)
2. William "Bill" Reresby Sitwell of Barmoor Castle FRGS (1916- ca. 2000)
3. Simon Talbot Sitwell DFC (1920-89)

After a couple of years of marriage Constance found that army life in India had palled and she was glad to return to England. Initially she lived for a short time with her mother in Hertfordshire, where she took up with the friends she had known as a young woman, before moving to Barmoor Castle, Northumberland.

Constance's friends came to stay at Barmoor Castle; they were mostly singers and painters. She preferred London because she found county gossip 'utterly boring.' She did not fit into the county social set and looked forward to the time she spent in the family's London residence where she would attend the tea parties of the Bloomsbury set. With her London friends she shared common interests and hardly a day passed without her having luncheon with one friend or another. She did not feel isolated, like she did when at Barmoor. In September 1932 she was with her husband when he died at Barmoor Castle.

Her numerous diaries never mention her having to deal with the problems of running a house – servants did everything. This afforded the ladies time to paint, write, socialise, and indulge themselves.

Constance wrote a number of books, the first was *Flowers and Elephants*.

A review stated that: *'Mrs. Sitwell has known India well, and has filled her pages with many vivid little pictures, and with sounds and scents. But it is the thread on which her impressions are strung that it is so fascinating, a thread so delicate and rare that the slightest clumsiness in definition would snap it. With an introduction by E.M. Forster'*

In *Literature of Travel and Exploration: An Encyclopedia*, (Taylor & Francis, 2003), Jennifer Speake writes: *British characterizations of the "romantic East" are ever present in travel writing. Flowers and Elephants (1927) is a typical example of this genre, depicting the fantastical East of the rajahs, rishis, and rituals that formed such a staple of the travel writing of British women during the empire. Constance Sitwell visits her brother, goes on an elephant ride, has tea with maharajahs, and idles in clubs. In a breathless survey of Indians and India she "envied them their beautiful tradition of clothes that goes on century after century unchanged." She observes the maharajah's male entourage: "With the deep far blue of the sky beyond them how amazingly vital they looked. Supple figures in shot green and gold, in pale shimmering blue and white, and on their heads high turbans of crimson and turquoise." She describes the thrill of being the guest of a Maharajah Rao Sahib of a "remote sandy State" or the killing of "Baloo, Baloo" (bear). Today the closest travel writers come to wild animals is through journeys in one of the many national parks that dot the country, and the splendour of Princely India is largely confined to the converted palace-hotels, of which the desert state of Rajasthan boasts many.*

Constance Sitwell's books were based on the material in her diaries. All had a concern with the continuity of life and the meaning of reality. She had a conviction that the life of the spirit was primary and had an expectation of joy and fulfilment after death.

The books she wrote were:

1. *Flowers and Elephants,* Jonathan Cape, 1927.
2. *Lotus and Pyramid*, Jonathan Cape, 1928.
3. *White Thorn, a Novel,* Pharos 1932.
4. *Petals and Places, a Novel,* Jonathan Cape, 1935.
5. *Bright Morning,* Jonathan Cape, 1942.
6. *Seek Paradise*, Jonathan Cape, London, 1948,
7. *Conversations with Six Friends,* Christopher Foss, 1959.
8. *Frolic Youth,* privately printed by Christopher Foss, 1964.

Note: This contains extracts from the author's diaries of almost sixty years before, including descriptions of everyday life at Renishaw, the seat of the Sitwell family.

9. *Bounteous Days*, Cecil Woolf, London, 1976

Note: Extracts from the author's diaries over the years 1913 to 1925.

10. *Smile at Time*.

She was for many years a member of the Society for Psychical Research and served on several of its committees. She had a great interest in Spiritualism and was President of the College of Psychic Science.

Dominic Montserrat refers to her in *Akhenaten: History, Fantasy and Ancient Egypt*, Routledge, 2000, p. 130:

In 1964 Constance fell on the ice outside Buckingham Palace and from then on she confined her living area to one floor of her London house until her death, ten years later. She died in October 1974 at the age of 87. A Memorial Service was held for her on 24th October, 1974 at St. Peter's, Eaton Square, London S.W.1.

SELECTED EXTRACTS FROM THE JOURNAL OF CONSTANCE SITWELL

India
January – March
1912

Edited by
John & Ann Ferguson

ARRIVAL IN BOMBAY

… The voyage out was so interesting that till we arrived at Bombay I had scarcely thought of what was coming at all. … Then we could see Bombay – could see the great city. There were drifts of smoke from the cotton mills in front, pinkish from the light of the rising sun, and out of them rose domes and towers – the tops lit by the golden light.

Passengers came and said good bye – I hate saying good bye to people. We landed after breakfast – some of the natives who had landed were garlanded. I could smell the smell which makes me drunk with delight – jasmine and temple-flowers. Nothing can be like the East but itself. Directly one is back one sees again what it is – how utterly, completely far away from anything but its wonderful intoxicating self. …

JAIPUR

… The city was all enclosed in great walls like those Indian cities are and everything inside was washed with a rose-pink wash. I thought it wanted a Tintoretto or a Titian to paint it, with its fantastic processions – and how it would have inspired Rossetti or William Morris.

The streets were straight and very broad, all round the city were blue hills, in between the pink houses moved the people in their flaming clothes. They wore brighter clothes there than at any other place we went to in India – at last one's hunger for colour was satisfied. To see men in vermillion velvet coats and cherry-coloured shawls and golden cap; streams of women in orange and pink and scarlet and rose, with copper and shining brass bowls on their heads and shining silver on their feet and arms; the little boys running in emerald satin and gold with embroidered crimson caps. Nobles rode down the street on ponies with high purple velvet saddles, orange leather harness and red ribbons fluttering, their retainers behind with swords and red saddles; even the white, meek-headed bullocks had their horns dyed a shrill green, the men had their beards dyed bright orange. If there was anything that could add colour it was them. There were peacocks on the pink sunlit walks real peacocks, moving slowly and painted peacocks standing with tail spread over dark doorways. The dyers dyed their cloth in the street – big brass bowls of saffron and sapphire and turquoise and scarlet. From the trees hung round bowls of water with green parrots fluttering thick round them. The green trees were full of those long emerald pointed wings and fast chattering. There were hosts of pigeons which made the open spaces blue when they all flew down, but what really melted me altogether were the flat baskets of marigolds and pink roses and jessamine that were set along the pavement and were being strung into garlands in the hot sun. ...

We went to the Palace. One couldn't go to the section where the family actually lived, but everywhere else. You drove first through the courtyards, with high high walls, and sort of cloisters all round where 'retainers' were sitting, and guards with rifles and swords on the ground beside them. From dark doors and through the gateways came the flaming people, men leading horses with brass trapping and bright red bows tied round their legs. The last courtyard had balconies round it, 'musicians galleries', and there were the musicians, sitting playing in the sun while the people moved slowly about below. Musicians looking down on to the sunny courtyard while they sang and played on long lutes and little drums, in turbans and scarfs and coats of pale blue and green and rose-coloured satin and silk, with silver bracelets and long ear-rings and toe-rings. How tremendously satisfactory it all seemed, that continual slow music, and the colours. Over the gateways were painted peacocks, and elephants charged each other on the pink walls. How new it was too, to see it going on now – instead of peopling dead places and one's imagination.

We were taken by our guide along dark marble passages to the armoury. Along the passages sat men making swords and sheaths, still making them as they had when wars were continual, the velvet sheaths embroidered with gold lay freshly finished on the marble. And then the armoury. How rich and dim it seemed, the worn Persian carpets and ceiling painted in squares, red and gold and royal blue and white, the old curved swords were in heaps, the scarlet and purple velvet sheaths lay piled one on another, long spears hung on the walls and, best of all, those richly painted long sticks in stacks of gorgeous colours.

And in another cool marble corner the 'scribes' were working – sitting copying from the old books, with lined, still faces, never looking up at us. Then we came to the picture-gallery. This family of Jaipur, one of the proud Rajput families, had been here for 600 years.

DELHI

… What I remember most about Delhi was driving out past old Delhi to the Persian poet's tomb – the little sunny pearly mosque surrounded by high sandstone buildings, and round it its marble courtyard with a row of gaily dressed musicians sitting in a row in front playing on their lutes and little drums, and singing in the sun, stretching up their arms and singing loudly and softly, and the rosy silken curtains that hung round, and the worn Persian carpets, and the twisted dark trunks of the mango trees and their pointed leaves, and the white tracery of carved marbles – the shadows delicate and clearly marked and splashed and heavy under the trees, the child in emerald velvet, and the men who sat by the white walls in vermillion and lilac and orange; Jehangira's grave covered only with grass and surrounded by eternal lilies and flowers of marble and the inscription upon it 'the humble and fleeting Jehangira – servant of the holy men and daughter of the emperor'. And in a further courtyard, shady with still trees, children playing quietly and old people sitting motionless and paraquets flashing across, was the poet's tomb, in a cool place and guarded by an old tall man, and heaped high – piled up with pink rose petals the lovely pale rose-petals – and the rosy shimmering curtains, the soft-footed people who came in humbly bowing and taking one petal away with them, the sound of musicians' voices, the warm warm air and white sunlight on white marble – and the still black shadows. I stood and looked and looked and rejoiced so in it. It seemed as if one had found Paradise.

LAHORE

… We plunged into Lahore gaiety and sport without a day's delay. The first afternoon we went and watched him playing polo. How new it all was – the dry polo-grounds and all the ponies being held by the syces, the young soldiers in white sun hats and fluttering shirts in the hot sun, one or two rather pale women looking on. Humphrey *(Constance's brother)* is a good, but rather violent player, I believe. He plays back for the regiment; he had 2 bright chestnut ponies, besides one other that was lame, and was a brave sight galloping and swerving about, sitting very erect, and pulling hard at the untrained ponies. They were cheaply bought, his ponies, and almost uncontrollable. They were called Hope, Faith and Charity for obvious reasons. (His hope and faith however were rather exhausted).

I had been longing to see what anglo-Indian life was like; it is extraordinarily like the books one reads about it – one almost felt as if one had lived it before. Through the genius of Kipling, I suppose. The people were very friendly and hospitable and frivolous – frivolous is a better word for them than gay. There were young men of every age and description, mostly soldiers or in the Civil Service and a few in the Police.

A new person arriving from England was the cause of a lot of comment and the socially-inclined person tried to be introduced as soon as possible. The young men lent one horses and saddles, and arranged rides on elephants, and got one invitations to dances and 'camp-fire concerts', and provided tea at sports, and drove one home from places in the dog-carts, and were extraordinarily nice generally. There was a big place called 'The Gymkhana' where everybody repaired at about 6 o'clock, then a band played and they

danced. It was a beautiful hall, and one sat and watched
men in white-flannels and polo-breaches, and all sort of
clothes, dancing with ladies in habits or white tennis shoes –
and the real nobs in tight-fitting satin dresses and big hats.
The people used to dress very smartly sometimes. At one
end was a refreshment bar where you got coffee and little
plates of chipped potatoes, and stuff called gram which you
ate with your fingers, and your friends also ate from the
same plate. What fun it all was. The people who had been
playing polo came in there and after riding one stopped there
in white sun-hat and hot habit and all the people came and
talked and arranged things – while the band played, and
outside the syces waited with dog-carts and horses, and the
evening air was fragrant. …

I shall never forget the first day's hunting. We had to start
at 5.45. We went in what is called a 'philton-gharry' – meant
to hold four – but we picked up 3 others besides ourselves
en route. It seemed so odd to me to set off in highest starlight – in sun hats. … It was quite cold. We passed one or
two horsemen whom everyone screamed at, and when we
got to the place of the meet there were dozens of ponies
waiting. … We stood on the bridge over the canal, and
Humphrey introduced me to dear Col: Sitwell, who was on
the Staff and the terror of all the 'young officers' and who
now stands out to me as the person who coloured India for
me. Afterwards I knew him very well. We used to ride
together, and talk together for hours and hours. All that I

know of soldiering or what war is like, or of marches and strange tribes and exploration and the desert, I learnt from him. ...

All the soldiers, except a very few in the Fort in the city, lived at the Cantonment which was about four miles from Lahore. An unattractive place – dry – and all the bungalows the same. It was just like a Kipling book to me. Col: Sitwell lived at the Cantonment, or Mian Mir as it was called. When we had been at Lahore about 10 days I saw him out hunting, and he asked me if I would come and stay with him, together with Mother whom he had never seen. I longed to go, to stay in a soldier's bungalow at the Cantonment would be great fun, I thought, and after suitable conversations we went there....

'Fort Lahore' what a grim-sounding name I used to think it when I wrote to Humphrey there. It is enormous, with the same regal splendour of the other forts built by those kings among kings, the Moghuls. There is a broad green ditch in between the two huge walls which used to be moat and now is smooth grass where parrots fly in shrieking hosts, and the English soldiers look down into it from the top of the towering red walls. In the Fort at Lahore is stored enough food to keep the whole of the English population of Lahore for 6 months and enough to feed the garrison for 7 years. Its guns are always trained, one on the water-works, one on the college, one on the telegraph-office. How tight is the bow string pulled there – at any moment the arrow can be loosed. Always there are soldiers in the Post Office, always an armoured train in the station. The station itself is built for defence, towers and slits to shoot through and provisions stored there and soldiers living there; everyone knows where they have to go at the word. Any morning hearing the alarm 'other than fire' each knows his place; one begins to feel the tension after a time, although it is not very acute, but there is that readiness in the air. Always the regiments march to church armed and with ammunition, and one evening when we were with Col: Sitwell and heard a lot of galloping down the hard road how he ran out to find out what it was, and we went too, and found all the servants already out there, and other doors open, and people looking. It was only the gunners coming back very late from some sports – but it might have been ---

AMRITSAR

One Sunday Mother and I went to Amritsar – we wanted to see the Golden Temple very much. It is the great place of the Sikhs. … We drove through the city in the motor, a most comic thing it was. … The motor could just go down the street without falling into the ditch each side, but there was no room for a person so they had to either flee before us or jump on to the counters on the shops or, very popular, take refuge in the ditch. The sacred bulls and goats that wandered along had to be pushed by force up little alleys and yards, we never knew if we shouldn't come face to face with something

– in which case no one knows what would have happened as we certainly could not turn round. It was fun. Lots of the inhabitants followed us along, and gave advice – "Olé, baboo" – one called if one wanted to attract a man's attention – "Listen – oh, scribe".

The Golden Temple was an amazing place and very beautiful. It stood there all shining gold, in the middle of a square tank, approached by a wide marble causeway with gold lamps all along it. All round the tank was a very broad white marble terrace where people sat selling their scented jasmine wreaths and long garlands of marigolds. How wonderful it looked in the setting sun light – those gleaming white courtyards and shining walls – and the crowds of people, mostly in white and yellow and orange, with the big baskets of white and yellow flowers amongst them. Here and there a child in emerald green and sapphire velvet coat – and a heap of pink roses.

We were the only Europeans there. Inside the Temple itself was kept the sacred book, guarded by priests who sat there and took the people's offerings – who then went and washed in the water – the Pool of Immortality it was called. Pigeons flew about outside and in. Every bit of the temple was painted or carved and covered with gold. Bunches and garlands of marigolds covered the middle part of it. By the side sat a holy man swathed in dull blue, his turban, stuck through with steel daggers, was blue and his face like a mask – motionless, absolutely expressionless – his eyes were fixed and he looked as if he would sit there throughout eternity without a sign. His blue clothes, the blue pigeons fluttering round him, and round them the golden walls and golden and orange flowers. There were considerable treasures, but we didn't see them. It was an amazing place – the men touching the ground with their heads – and the Fakirs sitting only moving their eyes, some old musicians sitting on the ground played on in a sort of trance occasionally all bursting into a harsh singing – a sort of frantic singing that grew louder and louder and suddenly died. How odd, and somehow how right it seemed this long sitting in the temple – quite quiet – withdrawn utterly from everything around them, half torpid for a time and then this sudden exultation that seemed to bubble up unreasonably – and that moved one by its vehement spontaneousness.

There were lots of other holy tombs round about and we walked about, all garlanded thickly with marigold wreaths and carrying sort of night-lights made of sugar which the keepers of the temple had given us. How can it be described to one who hasn't seen – that timelessness of the east? How the people sit still so still, hour after hour, and how right it seems – how all our arguments for action and movement dissolve and dissolve and you can't make them serve out there. Along the cool marble paths they sat, white against white walls, some looking, some only dreaming, holy men sitting in shrines blessing water for the passers-by, some of them with coarse faces, very much of the earth earthy, but one or two how calm and clever, one with a face like a wise Voltaire, wrapped in his salmon-coloured robes ...

BIKANER

We spent four or five days at Bikaner. It is a desert state in Rajputana, we travelled a day and a night to get there through desert. It was a narrow gauge railway and the sand blew in and stifled you if you opened the windows, also the glare was blinding, so the windows had to be kept shut and one lay along the leather seat in the melting heat of mid-day. One comfort we had – a huge basket of grapes, pomegranates, oranges, cape-gooseberries and guavas which Col: Sitwell had provided us with. We were the only European passengers – as Bikaner has no hotel – so if you go at all you go as the Maharajah's guest. It was a business train and Humphrey walked from his carriage to ours outside in pyjamas and a sun-hat. About 4 we arrived.

Bikaner is like a bit of Egypt set in the Indian desert. There were the thick low mud walls, and the tawny houses with a wooden camel saddle hung over the wall outside – and everywhere camels. ...

I never heard anything but praise for this man *(the Maharajah)*. He is A.D.C. to the King *(George V)* – when he is in India and also when he goes to England for any great occasion. He is quite young about 30, and is a good soldier and governs his desert kingdom in a model way. His camel corps has fought for us in China and in some other war, commanded by the Maharajah, who was only a boy in those days. He has such fine taste too. We saw some buildings, and terraces, and towers he had designed – graceful, Indian buildings. He also designed the uniforms for his cavalry, his body-guard, and the camel corps. Pale blue and silver, with pointed scarlet pennons for the cavalry, and for state occasions the camel corps glows in orange and red. All officials or anyone connected with the state wear those glowing orange turbans.

We were to dine at the Palace that night. ... It is a beautiful building, quite modern. One passed through great gates first and came upon the huge front of it, with the flag flying. Col: Wake in white uniform came and met us on the steps and we went through the hall, with its splendid white marble seats, into a great courtyard open to the sky; it seemed like bright moonlight there but was really lit by huge electric standards on the palace roof. There was a carpet in the middle, with a ring of chairs set around, and we sat there in the warm air – and the stars so bright above. All round were the galleries and stone screens of the palace. "Many eyes are looking down at you, and criticising every movement from behind those screens" said Col: Wake. So strange it seemed, and quiet. And then the young Maharajah came out into the white light of the courtyard, dressed all in white. We all fell victim to him, everybody does, the English that live there are most enthusiastic of all. He has such a pleasant voice, and all the time one is thinking with our English insularity, "What a gentleman he is – how courtly he is".

There were only a very few people at dinner, two of them his cousins dressed in tight dark blue uniforms. We all talked at dinner as if we were all old friends. … After dinner we went and looked at the different rooms. There were photographs of the King *(George V)* and Queen *(Mary)* and various royalties who had stayed there. It was odd to hear His Highness talk about the queen's dresses; "they are made of such beautiful stuff" he said "but always the same stiff style". He has ample opportunity of looking at them because he always stands by her at any function in India. The little boy held up her train with some other little princes all in satin and jewels. He was so proud of his palace that he had furnished in his own way so carefully. It was a satisfactory place. There were immense rooms with painted ceilings and dark carpets which had been made in the jail there. There were photographs of the two children on his writing-table, but none of either of the Maharanis. He had been married twice. His first wife had no children and he had married again, as is the Hindu custom. The two wives had each their bit of the palace to live in and sometimes called on each other, but didn't see each other much. He was equally fond of both, so they said, and thought the youngest the most beautiful woman in the world. Whenever he went away he brought back presents for them. They used to come in a covered in motor with him and watch the polo. Even Col:

Wake who had lived in the palace for about 3 years had never caught a glimpse of them, although he had been taken upstairs to places where he could be looked at nearby through little holes. The little girl who was about 11 years old never came out either, though when she was younger she used to ride and play about with her brother and Col. Wake. The Maharajah was tremendously fond of her and hated having to shut her up, but if he didn't no one would marry her. "The difficulties are too great" he said to his Mother … What a funny mixture it all seemed.

UDAIPOR

We arrived at Udaipor at 10 in the morning. It was the hottest place, and one of the most beautiful I have ever been in… If you want Medievalism you can find it there, and romance, and colour, and splendour. The Maharana is the proudest in India, his family have been there for 800 years and he is supposed to have descended from one of the (mythical Indian legends) children of the sun. "The other Majahs", he says, "are servants of the English King – I am his friend". He is not asked to do homage at the Durbar. He came and met the King at Delhi station, but beyond that nothing. At the last Durbar he sent his elephant, magnificently caparisoned but empty because he would not ride behind a woman (Lady Curzon). He speaks no English and will not have tourists and hardly would have the railway. He is a great sportsman and has killed 500 tigers. There are men posted on the top of the palace, and on the forts around, to signal if there is a tiger about and then the Maharana starts off to shoot it. In the evenings he goes to see the wild pig being fed by the side of the lake. He has no motors and is a Hindu; a sort of pope amongst the Hindus. He is the first gentleman in India – so to speak – the proudest of the Rajputs.

We drove to the dak bungalow, which is turned into a tiny hotel, along glaring white roads hedged with cactus, white with dust. It stood on a hill and from it one could see a towering mass of white towers and terraces high above the town – that was the Palace. It was too hot to move – we drank glass after glass of soda and lime juice, and read in the darkened room with every window and door tight shut to keep out the fiery air till tea-time. And then we drove out. What a place – a high wall all round the town, and double gates and guards with curved swords standing and sitting by, steep streets flaring white in the sun and streams of women like bunches of flowers each with a gleaming brass pot on her head going to the well. We came to a Hindu temple with great stone stairs leading down into the street, and at the top two great white elephants with raised trunks. All the time at Udaipor we only saw one European, so we were stared at a good deal at every point. An enormous Hindu, shining with oil and almost clothless stood at the top and smiled but motioned that we might not go in the temple. We might walk around it though and that was extraordinary enough. It towered up, tapering to a point, all grey stone and every inch was carved. Freiezes of elephants and then a frieze of horses, eternally rearing stone horses and riders, and the men and monkeys and grotesque heads, up and up and up they looked down on you. The Boy, who is a Hindu, watched in amazement with open-mouthed delight. It was his show, so to speak. Standing there alone, and seeing those gigantic blindingly white elephants against that azure sky and the white steps in front of them going down and down – one couldn't forget it . And then we drove on up the steep street to the first gates of the Palace. Up narrow paths and stone steps we climbed and, looking over the wall, suddenly saw far below the lake – bright blue, and on every little island a graceful white water palace, all colonades and towers and balconies and cupolas, softly shining in the sun and, all round, the high hills crowned with high walled forts. There was the beach where the wild pigs were fed every evening, and had been for 200 years, and there was another bit of yellow sand where groups of women were sitting and wailing. A man had died and had been burnt and, as the guide said, "woman's cryings". And then we came to the Palace. Guards in old uniforms were sitting in the marble cloisters round the courtyards with their curved swords by them.

There was the treasury with open doors and more guards. There was a long square garden surrounded by marble terraces and carved marble columns – all white – and how beautiful the men were who leaned against them in orange or lilac or pink. Looking out of any marble window you saw the sunny town far below and the deep blue lake. There were many rooms, painted and with glass and one made of blue china. There was a courtyard which had splendid enamel peacocks all round it, radient creatures with their slender heads bent forward so smooth and glowing, sapphire and emerald. And we stood on carved balconies and walked down dim marble stairs and passages, and so till we came onto the gigantic broad terrace where the Maharana can parade his whole army, elephants and all. It was evening now and all the chickens and geese and pigs were being fed at one corner, camels and horses and bullocks were being led out and in. A dancing horse with a pink velvet cloth over it was being led up and down by a man in scarlet, and prancing about. This was for the Maharani to look at out of the window. It is a marvellous place, perfectly medieval, as we came down into the town again we met some nobles galloping up the slope to the palace, red ribbons fluttering on their horses, and the retainers behind with swords. Sometimes they have a falcon on their wrists The proud features and high turban with the ends streaming out behind – what splendid creatures they look. And the poetry of it too. The golden sun that shines on the palace wall with the face of a man and the great light which is lit at night and which has round it 'Heaven's light be our guide'.

The Maharana is an ascetic man and rules his people with justice and great care. Whenever he rides through the town he gives a silver coin to every woman he meets. He has only been married once, his only son is a cripple. There was a picture of him, a boy with a pathetic and sensitive face. And there was also a picture of the Maharana when he was younger, in black with a long sword, a proud small head and dark eyes and one row of big pearls round his neck.

The next morning we were up early. By 7 we were down on the steps which lead down to the lake. There were grey steps all along, and boats, green and yellow boats, and one barge painted bright pink which took the royal family to the water-palaces. They lived in these in the hot weather. They do know how to live. They do dream beauty and achieve it and live in it – they are artists, and poets, they seem to me an amazing chivalrous, romantic race.

Early morning by the lake, cool and quiet, and the flowering trees and fragrant flowers. We were rowed along to one palace after another, white palaces with marble steps and pillars, and in front of one of them a row of vast grey stone elephants standing above the little turquoise ripples with trunks uplifted. What many delights were there. ...

The Goanese hotel-keeper, having no other guests came and saw us off at the station – one of the horses of the conveyance fell down on the way, amidst great excitement. Some toy sellers took advantage of the stop however to sell us some nice painted toys. A mongoose ran across the road, I remember, from dusty cactus hedge to dusty cactus hedge. The Boy who had started hours before in a bullock cart with the luggage had just arrived at the station.

FLOWERS AND ELEPHANTS

We never saw a European all the time at Udaipor. This day it was Sunday and we heard a little bell. There were four English inhabitants, the hotel-keeper said, and that bell was for their church. All that night, and all the next day we spent in the train. Those Indian nights – when one looked out of the window hour by hour, singing old songs and hymns, while the air got cooler, and Canopus rose and rose over the mysterious land, and the faint stars of the False cross trembled over the horizon. How wonderful they seemed to me, charged with emotion and strange passion, 'Is not the night our cup – are not the stars our wine'. The immense night, inarticulate and sombre, with its silence, its fragrant and stifling breath, its deep repose, and all the sounds that come, of that life – timeless and vast – which wakes at night. The world is drunk, is drunk with night, sometimes I wished that they would never end.

AGRA

... We drove through the town, and as it got clearer, and the moon was rising we drove straight on to the Taj. Before one gets there one is ready to carp and criticise and be slightly contemptuous. One is so sick of hearing about it, of reading of it, of seeing pictures and photographs and models of it; one doesn't know. Because the architecture is not so very fine, it is very near being decadent, it is not virile in any way. All that, one can say. But still it remains more sweet, more dreamy, more loving almost than anything you had imagined before.

[190]

FLOWERS AND ELEPHANTS

It was faint moonlight when we got there and coming through the big sandstone gateway saw it - silence falls on you when you see it. Nothing has quite prepared you for its peace, it pearly serenity and calmness. It is intimate, and yet mysterious – like the woman, perhaps, it was built for. It seems as if it could only have been built by a lover for his love. There is a lotus pond in the middle of the garden where the marble paths meet, and from where the water-courses flow. The cypresses stand sentinel straight along each path, at the end raised on a marble platform is the Taj – with terraces on each side. You go up many white steps before you go into that amazing interior with its sandlewood doors which scent all the dim place.

There is a light always burning over the tomb of the Queen, which is in the middle, such a little tomb it looks, and the King was buried afterwards by her side. There they lie, close to each other in the scented wonderful dim light under the pearly dome. Lilies and roses, poppies and convolvuli, iris and graceful colombines, creepers and jessamine always blooming round them, eternally soft and brilliant set in the pure marble and the marble screen around them! Can stone be made so soft and living, and full of grace and tenderness? The air is so sweet, the light is so softly sweet.

On her grave are piled pink roses and rosy oleanders, and the starry jessamine that she loved so much. Outside the Jumma flows calmly on, a broad flood far below the white terraces, palm trees on its far side, buffaloes with meek heads standing quiet in the water and two boys singing on the banks. You can't talk much at the Taj. The moonlight got clearer and brighter, the domes seemed to float, it all seemed veiled with light, and it stuck one with awe. I stood and looked in silence as if in a vision, a mystery put into this beautiful form for the beautifying of one's soul. Who can help indeed not being uplifted when men have dreamed and achieved such things as some of these Indian kings? Beauty of love, beauty of devotion, beauty of soul, beauty of life and death.

FATIHPUR SIKRI

The next day we went to Fatihpur Sikri, the City of Victory. Akbar built it when his son was born, it is built on a ridge in an immense plain. No one but the Saint Salim Cristi lived there till Akbar built his glorious royal city, which for 25 years was the centre of roaring life. (At the end of that time for no reason we can give, he left it, and never went back).

Here he collected poets and sculptors, philosophers and artists, doctors, saints, soldiers, statesmen; himself the greatest soldier, the purest statesman, the bravest thinker, the most daring sportsman and the best musician of them all. Akbar, the Emperor, slim, and full of dreams. I shall never forget the day we went to Fatihpur Sikri. ... The morning had been intolerably hot. From 10 o'clock till one I wandered about our big room trying to pack with very few clothes on, continually sipping iced lemonade and standing between any window or door where any sort of tiny draft blew. It was stifling and the red dust blew chokingly about in the bare yard outside where the servants slept in the shade. And then thunder rolled, and a few drops of rain, such heavy heavy drops on the roof. Then the wind blew fiery hot again, and more thunder, and the parched leaves fell, and dust – round and round in little columns danced about outside and then the rain splashed down. Poured and splashed and beat and fell down, the dust was all red mud. Oh the coolness and fragrance of the earth, the ground churned, the roads little rivers with the drops falling deep into them. It was time for us to start, we were all ready sitting on the verandah, the sky so long vacantly blue was heavy purple grey, and flying clouds. It hypnotised one, such rain as that. One watches and feels it in a sort of trance - the water that poured off the roofs and beat down the flowers, the clouds that were torn and torn again by the swift blue lightening. The motor that was to take us stood there under the porch, painted yellow, in a sea of mud. Rain like that has to abate sometime. When it got a little less heavy we got ourselves capes and rugs and settled ourselves in. ...

At last we got to gateways and ruined walls and city walls and fortifications, and were at the great dead city. How wet the ground was, how red the palaces stood up against the dark grey sky, how the forked lightening flickered and ran about the sky. There was not one soul there except ourselves. ... I wish I had kept all my epithets of wonder and praise unused, so as to be able to praise this Gate of Victory aright, for surely it is the most royal, the most majestic thing in the world? The Pyramids of Karnak – they move one to awe – but this gate, so beautiful, so pathetically grand standing on the top of its tremendous flight of steps, opening to a dead city, it moves one to tears. The sky was weeping that day and one sobbed almost with the sorrow and pathos of it all. I stood on the top of those steps which led down down into the plain, from there you could see mile beyond mile of India. The great gateway towered up into the sky, built of red sandstone surmounted by pillars and white domes, so full of dignity, so regal, a superb idea and one which only a genius like the Emperor could put into being. And around this great gate of Victory what words are written? Are they proud words of glory – as indeed they have more reason to be than on any other building in the world? What are the words that Akbar had set there, in black marble for everyone who came in to read? 'Said Jesus, on whom be peace: The world is a bridge. Pass over it, but build no house therein. He who hopes for an hour hopes for eternity. Spend the hour in prayer. The rest is unknown'.

I stood there under the balconies where Akbar used to sit in the evenings and look out over the vast plain fading to blue and the lightening blinded one every other minute and the rain beat down. Mother was frightened of the thunder and had taken refuge in some palace, and I was there alone. How grandly those great steps rose out of the plain above the deserted houses, so royal and no one to see it – so towering and no one to wonder at it, so vast and no one to pass through into the great court yard. How quiet it was - and not a soul anywhere to be seen. I grew almost frightened at its grandeur, and its deadness.

I went up some dark stairs in the wall and on to a broad terrace on to the roof, all wet with rain. This is where Akbar walked in the evenings. Imagination grew so strong in that silent place that it seemed to me I could almost see him – as if I was passing him on the dark stairs, my heart beat so I rushed away across the open space all surrounded by cloisters and halls and palaces, with the perfect mother-of-pearl tomb built for the saint *(Salim Cristi)* in the middle, and found Mother standing under one of the broad gateways. What a place to wander in.

We saw the 'Hall of dreams' where he used to sleep his short night and where each night a philosopher would be summoned to discourse with the Emperor. We saw the hospital he built, the long ornamented palace for Birbal, his minstrel friend, we saw the gateway with colossal elephants each side whose trunks met over the top. We could hear the peacocks, and see the grass growing between the stones which paved the paths. Oh splendid King, how hard I tried to see your city as you must have seen it; the figures in crimson and scarlet and gold, the painted elephants, and horses with harness of silver and gold, the children with wreaths of flowers on their head singing the song of the

dawn, the incense, and music and jewels, the heavy
gorgeousness of it all, the riches and splendour and luxury.
And you coming, rose leaves and jessamine scattered before
you, dressed always in white, always aspiring, always reaching
out to something higher, always seeking for Truth. 'It is Thou
I seek from Temple to Temple'. ...

HOMEWARD BOUND

We left for Bombay that morning; we had a 'Durbar carriage'
to ourselves. It was upholstered in blue satin and had six
electric lights and fans, and a table and all sorts of luxuries.
Nothing however could keep out the heat. We passed
Gwalior, the immense ochre-coloured Fort burning in the
sun – and saw the white towers of the palace. We went
through jungle (or rather rukh) and passed miles and miles
of coral trees – glowing – and a mist of red when further
away. The last night in the train, when the little beds were
made and your night-gown on and the windows open – to
lie and look out at the plains in the moon-light, at the broad
rivers we passed over, so low that all the flat rocks were
uncovered, 'Peace rocks' (and I imagined Hathi standing there
in the quiet light of the moon, and Shere Khan coming to
drink and Mowgli sitting cross-legged by the bank). How
very exciting it all was. The time in India was over though,
and all its sights and smells and sounds seemed to be so
dear.